This book is dedicated to many of those who have inspired me in life:

My co-author, Pastor Bob Brock whose Biblical insights, kindness and dedication are an inspiration to me.

My co-author and long time friend Reggie Brock, who carries our mission to help others deeply in his heart.

My mentors in business, Susan and Dwight Havener, who never cease to amaze and inspire me by their consistent dedication to those around them.

My father and mother, Samuel and Dena Mastrangelo and sister, Sharon, who have always encouraged me to live and walk in faith.

My spiritual sounding board and friend,
Stevyn Muller and his wife Lori who have
sustained us in prayer.

My dear wife Tina, who encourages me
daily, through her example and love, to
strive to be the man of God I desire to be
with my whole heart.

To God be the glory for all the things He
has done and for my wonderful family and
friends.

Foreword

The Story of the Brook

This is a page from the life of Elijah the prolific prophet of God. It is recorded in I Kings 17: 2-16.

After Elijah prophesied that a severe drought was going to fall upon the entire country and that economic conditions were going to plummet, God sent him to hide at Cherith until the anger of the people subsided.

As conditions worsened, God commanded wild birds to cater three square meals a day to him to provide nourishment for his body and gave him a brook from which he could drink to give him fluids to keep him alive.

One day, to his surprise, the birds did not make their food delivery and the brook gradually began to dry up and finally went dry.

His days were numbered until God once again spoke and commanded him to go to Zarephath of

Sidon where he would meet a widow woman that would become the vehicle of God to meet his needs. As he entered the gates of the city, he met the widow woman who was gathering sticks to build a fire so that she could cook one last meal for her and her son.

Elijah asked her to feed him as well, but she told him that she had only enough meal and oil for one last meal and none extra to spare. He assured her that if she would extend the hospitality of a meal to him that her meal barrel would never be empty and her oil jar would never drain down to the last drop.

She did him the favor, and the miracle of God's divine provisions came to pass.

Contents

Introduction

Newly married just six months, twenty-five years old and my husband, a top salesman for a Fortune 500 company came home and said "I can't do this anymore. I can't go to that job. They let John go today. He has had such a rough time of it with his wife being ill and dying and his territory cut back. They are going to continue to cut the territories. It's not going to get better. I've got to do something else."

That day changed our lives forever. There have been amazing ups and horrendous lows since that day, but through it all our faith in God's plan for our lives and our belief in the network marketing industry have been strengthened over and over again. Because of what we have been through we want to share with others our faith and to help others achieve what the Lord has set before them.

Both David and I were raised in God fearing Christian homes and were blessed with loving parents who instilled the love of Jesus in us. We have both strayed far away from the path many times, but have always come back to the Lord. Today we have faith, because of our trials and tribulations, which withstands the little things and has begun to prepare us for a world that is going to need strong believers.

That day in March of 1993 I didn't really know what to say except "O.K. so what do you think you want to do?" Talk about blind faith. David then said, "network marketing." I had no idea what that was, but marketing sounded good and I knew he had strong sales skills. He had been introduced to network marketing many years before we met. He had been 'garage certified', a term I learned to understand, and worked with a company for a little while, but never really worked it as a bread and butter business. I didn't have a clue, but he introduced me to the concept through a few friends and we began on our journey. Let me tell you, as soon as I was introduced to the business, I made it clear that this was his business. I was a speech-language pathologist with a passion for my hospital work and had no, repeat no, 'sales' skills or desire to sell anything. On the other hand, David was a natural. He is bold with his faith and bold talking to people. But, I was supportive. I encouraged him to do what he needed to do. I would go to meetings with him, take the products and I enjoyed the first cruise he won immensely.

But, the happy ending network marketing success story didn't begin or end with the cruise. Without solid mentors, without a company that had integrity the income faltered. Bonuses were great and we loved the product because we felt healthy and lost weight, but between buying products and qualifying people and advertising, the checks didn't cover the expenses and we were accruing credit card debt to keep us in the race.

After winning the cruise, but not having money to spend on the side trips, and having dedicated a year and a half to the attempt, David knew he had to do something else. He began researching other companies, still believing in the concept. We signed up in another company and within six months had reached the top of the pay plan. We had income now that was paying the bills. What a relief, but then again a speed bump was before us. The company was not all we had believed it to be and we knew that we again had to look elsewhere.

Then we were blessed beyond measure. As David was trying to recruit a couple, the couple recruited him. Again, a night that changed our lives forever. He came home and said a little sheepishly, I think he would even admit, "Honey, we've joined another company." But from that day on, his sponsors spent time with him, guided him, mentored him to achieve success. It was no longer a business of getting people to sign up and see who would take off. It became a career of helping others look at the industry in different ways, as a passion, as a service, as a money making business. From here David became what most would consider as not only successful, but dramatically successful. Within six months through his hard work and dedication and with their solid mentoring, our income exploded, the debt was paid off almost overnight and we were well past the point where people would say we were successful network marketers living the dream of financial and time freedom. Yes, you heard me say "we". As I saw David's success, saw the benefit of the industry to others, experienced story after story from non-salesman, preachers, housewives, teachers, construction workers, waitresses, nurses, literally anyone you could imagine, my belief soared. Even to this day, I've never given up my speech pathology career because I love it, but I now realize that anyone can do this business and be successful given the right tools and support. Now, I also consider myself along with David to be one of the many blessed to be called a network marketer. We became a team in the business. He trains, guides and mentors and I am the support system wherever and whenever he needs me.

And we all lived happily ever after? No. David went through an incredibly hard time after the passing of his father, Sam. They were best friends and even though we know that Sam, a strong man of God, knew the Lord and is with Him now, the loss impacted David's drive to work the business. What most people do not know or understand or really believe about the network marketing business is that it really provides long-term residual income and it is a complete 'real' business. Many would not understand why with a successful business we would sell the business or even that we could sell it and in retrospect some days we also wonder, but remember God has to take you through things to put you where He wants you to be spiritually and physically. We sold our business and a close friend, spirit filled Christian brother and vice-president of a company asked David to run his sales team. Sales increased and the two of them determined that working together could be just what they both needed and the industry reentered our lives. They started a consulting company and began building systems for individual networkers and companies to be successful on the internet, began writing for network marketing magazines, and authored training and seminar materials. Through these avenues David became a respected trainer and consultant with many network marketing companies at the corporate level. What insights the Lord has given him! What experiences he has had, and what faith has been built!

We have been brought back full circle through every avenue of this industry. Today we envision our mission as assisting others in achieving the greatness we believe God has prepared for His children. We now walk like few others have had the opportunity to walk, in God given spiritual discernment and human experience, insight, and faith in an industry that provides opportunity for the masses like no other. Through over fifteen years of the roller coaster of network marketing we have seen the potential of people and the industry to create what they desire if they have the guidance and direction that is needed, and if they take the opportunity on as a personal challenge and mission. We have seen individuals regardless of age, education, nationality, experience or skills who have achieved full-time incomes in the industry in a multitude of companies. We have seen individuals who have achieved dramatic incomes within months of joining a company and individuals who have achieved those full-time incomes through daily, consistent work over years. What I'm sharing with you is not everyone will be successful, not everyone who becomes successful will create success the same way, but having traveled the road with hundreds of thousands of other home-based business owners, we tell you the potential is great. What a journey, what a blessing He has provided us with!

Throughout the journey whether on the mountain or in the valley, we have strived to remain true to our Christian heritage of love, caring, helping, serving, ministering, tithing, honesty and not going anywhere our Lord and Savior, Jesus Christ, has not led us. We have not always succeeded, but we continue to pray our way through. We hope that our journey and direction will assist you as you read these chapters to see the Lord's will in your life and if He leads you down this path that you will see the blessings that this industry can provide.

To you the spouse:

To answer those questions of "What is my husband or wife doing?" "Is he or she crazy?" "Is this a waste of time and money?" Without a doubt, I confidently tell you that their potential is great. All they need is your support along the way, don't hold them back, encourage them, support them, love them, honor them and respect them for their entre-preneurial spirit and most of all pray that their God given abilities will be utilized. You can be the difference in whether or not they remain in the status quo or whether they achieve God given success as my wonderful David has done. **There is no doubt in our minds that when one brook dries up, God can turn your situation into blessing!**

— Tina Mastrangelo

Chapter 1

Status Quo Has Got To Go!

It is not impossibilities, which fill us with the deepest despair, but possibilities, which we have failed to realize. — Robert Mallet

The old grey mare ain't what she used to be. She will never run the Kentucky Derby or accept out sourcing contracts from the John Deere tractor giant again. She served her purpose and has been retired to the pasture. WHAT WORKED EFFECTIVELY AND PROFITABLY YESTERDAY MAY NOT WORK TODAY. No one knows this better than Elijah (I Kings 17). His brook had been an unfailing source to sustain him during a severe economic downturn. He was comfortable and confident that Old Faithful would provide, but one day the water level began to recede and soon it was all dried up.

It is plain to see that many people's brooks today are drying up also. Unemployment could soar from 6% to over 15%. Underemployment is another disappointing issue. According to a national news release, a corporate executive who was earning around a half million dollars a year got booted off the corporate ladder and is now delivering pizza to keep food on the table.

We once considered our home to be not only our castle but a very good, safe investment, but many are realizing dramatic declines in their property values. But in the face of drastic reality, we must not panic. The psychology of fear only adds fuel to the fire. We must plan, pray and pursue opportunities from previously rejected or even unconventional sources as viable options.

This may surprise you, but *when the economy goes down the interest in network marketing goes up.* People look away from their brooks. When recession hits, people scramble to find alternative sources of income and provision. In their frantic searches, they are finding that network marketing may be one of the best of all alternatives for many because of its availability, low start up cost, low maintenance, low risk and positive income potential.

As in the chronology of Elijah's life, old methods immediately became obsolete. *Status quo had to go. The brook was gone.* Elijah was forced to change. His survival depended upon it. God was moving him on, changing him, and directing him away from the status quo. Rest assured God never closes one door without opening another. The fact remains ever the same. God makes opportunities for us, but He expects us to hunt for them and invest sweat equity in them if need be. Through each situation, He wants us to grow.

Our hold back is that it is easier for us to go hunting for economic dinosaurs in our own back yards. Its familiar territory, and who wants to leave their comfort zone? We hope to stay safe, comfortable and accidentally stumble over a financial opportunity and new income stream without stretching our imagination, looking for a new idea or working too hard. Ironically, financial opportunities often are found in someone else's yard, just outside the box and may be disguised in fancy duds of creative, innovative ideas that are not fashionable.

Jeremiah espoused this idea and encouraged those within his sphere of influence to *"break up your fallow ground, and sow not among thorns."* (Jeremiah 4:3) What an interesting challenge in interesting economic times! The word "fallow" means land that has been left unplanted and inactive. It could well mean doing something with land that has gone unnoticed and untouched for whatever the reason. The implication is obvious. Status quo must go. Now is the time to open our eyes to new opportunities, to some of the finest products and services available, to new income streams, and to learning new skills. **The network marketing industry provides what many may need right now.**

Elijah also had to discover new resources in a culture where distrust was the norm and not the exception. Initially, he had to accept and feel confi-

21

dent that he could not continue to maintain a status quo and become successful. He must think of alternatives and take action outside of the box.

Moving from the secluded lifestyle of Cherith, a seaside village on the Mediterranean, to the foreign city of Zareapath in the country of Jezebel, his greatest opposition of the time, was like walking into a hornet's nest. It looked unrealistic and dangerous. Consequently, to act in obedience and follow the Lord's guidance required no less than rethinking his whole basic value system. It takes a big man to do that.

According to the custom of that era, going to this economically destitute widow woman was going against the grain of uniform conduct. His masculinity was being threatened and years of tradition were being trampled under his feet. This plan was not one with which he could immediately resonate. This was a Gentile widow woman, and to go to her for help was an ultimate form of condescension. It would not have been too unusual for him to ask help of a Jewish widow, as the presence of a man would add status or a sense of stability to her home. When God sent him to a Gentile woman's home, normalcy was abandoned and the blessing was amplified. Conventional thinking got trashed and his primary focus changed. He was forced to accept a new method that was designed by God for that page in history.

Network marketing is much like that. **Preconceived ideas limit us from having open minds to what may be God's provision for us.** Consequently, our biggest problem is the six inches between our ears. I wish that we could be as observant and honest as the college guy who realized that he was about to flunk a class and tried to explain it to his parents with this note. "I have a clinker in my thinker." Status quo is the 'clinker' in our thinker to many of us.

The Bible addresses the importance of our thinking in Proverbs 23:7. *"For as he thinketh in his heart, so is he…"* Paul was equally emphatic about having a *mind miracle*. In Romans 12:2 he wrote, *"And be not conformed to this world; but be ye transformed by the renewing of your mind, that you may prove what is that good, acceptable, and perfect will of God."* The good, acceptable and perfect will of God can only be discovered when a transformation takes place in our mind and the outcome that most of us desire in our lives will never be realized until our thinking changes. Status quo thinking must go.

Paul raised the bar in thinking God's way in Ephesians 3:20. He wrote: *"Now unto him that is able to do exceeding abundantly above all that we ask or think, according to the power that works in us."* You can't out think God. Think big, and you will be thinking like God.

Peter learned this lesson the hard way. In Acts 10:14, he was rather *defiant* when God spoke to him in terms that he did not understand or with which he did not agree. God said, *"Rise, Peter; kill and eat. But Peter said, Oh no Lord. I've never so much as tasted food that was not kosher. The voice came a second time: If God says it's okay, it's okay. (The Message)."* Peter must have been a slow learner because Jesus had previously pounded this truth into his head as recorded in Matthew 16:23. He said, ***"You stand right in my path, Peter, when you look at things from man's point of view and not from God's** (Phillips translation)."* What a divine revelation! Good, Godly people can unwittingly stand in God's way by seeing things solely from their own vantage point and disregarding how God sees it. Bias can be blinding and binding.

You talk about tough love. The words of Jesus were strong. Jesus told Peter that he said what God told him to do was wrong, but God says it is okay and when God says it is okay-it is okay. To do otherwise is to stand in God's way and prevent Him from doing what He wants to do in your life. Seek and find your okay from God and follow it.

Read it again. *"…When you look at things from man's point of view and not from God's."* This was the problem. Peter had a knack of looking at things from a human vantage point. I pray that God will help you to take a look at the principles of network marketing, see them as they are, and if He says "it's okay", it's okay, and then let go of the status quo.

Going beyond status quo in the industry will require you to make a few logical investments. You will need to invest in your vision, your belief level, your knowledge base, and your commitment to being your own boss.

#1. Invest in your Vision.

Vision is the ability to see things even though they do not yet exist. *"Now faith is the substance of things hoped for, the evidence of things unseen."*

24

(Hebrews 11: 1) **Visions drive us to do things we never believed we could do before. They drive us when we hesitate to go beyond status quo.**

Henry Ford dreamed of a time when the average American would be able to afford to drive their own automobile. He envisioned a plan to make cars affordable. That vision resulted in mass production of affordable cars for the working class.

Investing in your vision entails taking consistent action to begin to build what does not yet exist.

Limiting your vision will limit your ability to get beyond the status quo. So…think big! Consider the examples of Ray Kroc who franchised the first McDonald's in 1954, and Walt Disney who met a childhood actor named "Mickey" Rooney and then named a little cartoon mouse he created after him. Were they crazy for dreaming big?

You have to see yourself out of debt with limitless income potential. Envision yourself with time and money to do what you want. Embrace your vision and make consistent, persistent investment until your dreams become reality.

#2.Invest in your Belief Level.

Why is belief so important to getting out of the status quo? Because without belief, you have failed before you even started. What we believe dictates our actions. To become successful in network marketing you must believe in four key areas: the company, the products or services, the network marketing industry, and yourself. For many people the hardest one may be believing in themselves. What a hold of Satan it is that we as Christians, as children of an omnipotent father, doubt ourselves, pity ourselves, or hide behind our histories.

If self-confidence is a problem for you, begin with these basic actions:

- Get in the word of God and read about the mighty men and women of God who with all of their human faults still produced victories, overcame doubts, and achieved miraculous works. Don't put your faith in yourself or men, place it in God.
- Distance yourself from those who discourage you from pursuing your dreams.
- Spend time with those who believe in you, will motivate you to succeed and those who have already achieved success.
- Build your belief in your ability to succeed through partnering with a successful sponsor group.
- Take daily action such as three-way conference calls, so you can start seeing results. Results are the combatants to lack of confidence. You will be amazed at the self-confidence built with every new person you recruit. Excitement is an incredible motivator.

#3. Invest in your education and skills

Most of those who are successful in business have achieved through applying the things they know and persisting where others have given up. You can't expect to earn solid income without putting in study, practice and action. There is an old adage that says: "The more you learn, the more you earn." School is never out for the pro. Continue being a student of your profession. Learn all you can about how to do network marketing better!

In Proverbs 4:7-8 the wise man taught us about the supreme importance of wisdom and a continuing education when he said, *"Above all and before all, do this: Get Wisdom!"* Write this at the top of your list… I don't want you ending up in blind alleys, or wasting time making wrong turns. Hold tight to good advice; don't relax your grip. Guard it well—your future is at stake.

The disciples didn't become world changing overnight. They spent time with Jesus. They listened to the guidance He gave. They experienced the miracles He demonstrated. Then they were filled with the Holy Spirit and changed lives. What an example for us! **Unless a miracle occurs, most harvests come from applied efforts.**

#4 Invest in how to be self-employed.

When starting out especially with part-time hours, you MUST allocate time to action to build a full-time income. Few have the skills and financial support to stop what they are doing to meet their bills, put all their eggs into one basket and wait for the payoff. Unless you have no other option and currently can commit yourself full-time to building your business, then realize that becoming self-employed regardless of the industry you choose is better initiated one step at a time. **Companies providing immediate income for new business builders are the quickest way to replace current income. Companies providing percentages for building and developing leaders provide the ongoing income and residual that is the trademark accomplishment of the industry.** Plan your time to work your prospect list with your sponsor, to make follow-up calls with prospects and customers, and to have training calls with your new distributors.

Connecting with leaders and time for personal development must be planned. Where many new distributors fail is continuously "getting ready" to take action and never actually making the contacts. Many that are used to punching a clock and having their work day dictated by their boss lack the discipline needed to persist in the necessary actions. Just remember that if your appointment book is empty your pockets will be empty also.

Farmers understand that if you want something to grow you must plant seeds. Building a business requires consistent planting, which in this business is the investing of time and effort, making contacts and following up. This is the way to grow a crop, to achieve life beyond the status quo.

Jesse Jackson's son said it eloquently in nominating his father at the 1988 Democratic Convention: "The shame in life is not to fail to reach your dream, but to fail to have a dream to reach." Make your decision right now to let go, because status quo has got to go.

Chapter 2

Where was God when my brook dried up?

"For in glory He (GOD) is incomprehensible, in greatness unfathomable, in height inconceivable, in power incomparable, in wisdom unrivaled, in goodness inimitable, in kindness unutterable." -Theophilus of Antioch

This is not a burlesque show, but we are searching for the naked truth! There's so much garbled gook flying around out there that spins off more questions than it provides answers. As a result, many of us are in the same quagmire as was Pilate as he stood scratching his head in confusion standing before Jesus and asking, "What is truth?" He discovered, as do we, that truth is not always easy to come by. So how do we know truth and is God in it?

Millions are asking that same question today. What is the truth about the economy?

The question is not when will the brook dry up? The fact is that it already has for millions. Homes in foreclosure, jobs lost, and bankruptcies are screaming headlines in daily newspapers across the country. Unemployment lines are swelling at record-breaking speed, and retirees are being forced to go back to work to survive.

Senate Minority Leader Mitch McConnell (R-KY) has been employing a Bible-based comparison to explain our national debt. He describes it like this. "If you started the day Jesus Christ was born and spent $1 million every day since then, you still wouldn't have spent $1 trillion."

Senator John Thune (R-SD) hoped to make a lasting impression on our staggering national debt load by pointing out on the Senate floor that a trillion, one-dollar bills would make a stack 689 miles high.

Emily Thornton of Business Week made this fascinating observation. "America used to be the land of the free. Now it's the land of the fee." The ordinary working man and woman are "fee-ed" to death.

The truth is that many people today must find new sources of income. In Luke 5:4-10 Simon (Peter) had already worked hard the night before without a catch, but then Jesus said to him *"Now go out where it is deeper and let down your nets and you will catch a lot of fish!"* Nine to five jobs are not only becoming more and more scarce, but are also breeding grounds for insecurity, so we must "go out deeper and let out our nets." **Alternatives such as network marketing**

must be considered when the standard efforts aren't producing a catch.

Jesus made this shocking comparison between the children of this generation and the children of light, and I can almost still feel the heat from His words. *"For the children of this world are in their generation wiser than the children of light* (Luke 16:8)."* I must tell you that evaluation report from our all wise Lord makes my blood boil. Not at our Lord, but at the inept, indifferent mood of the church. It's an indictment against believers and churches to limit themselves and assume a position of being dumber than unbelievers. Jesus was declaring that the world is out-smarting us. They play hardball and we play ring around the roses. It is nothing short of an accusation with which we must plead guilty. It is a sharp call to arms and a challenge to wise up and out smart the devil. We not only can, but we must!

It's a tough place to be. Elijah did not find it easy to find truth when a sense of helplessness overwhelmed him and his economic and physical resources dried up (I Kings 17). We would be remiss to overlook the fact that he was where God sent him, doing what God had sent him to do and honoring God in explicit obedience. But his brook dried up. Trials and tribulations experienced for the Christian are faith builders, but certainly we may be asking, **"What is the next step when it happens to us?"**

Where was God when Elijah's world fell apart? Was his prophetic, ministry of miracles over? How could this happen to him here and now? This was not a lesson he learned in the school of the prophets. It was God's special word for him. New revelation was needed for a new crisis. The Bible says, *"And the word of the Lord came to him…"* (KJV-I Kings 17:8) Where was God? He was close enough to speak to him in this crisis and give him a way out. God always has a way out. It may not look right or feel right, but it is always right if it comes from God. The prophet of old was correct when he wrote, *"For the ways of the Lord are right, and the just shall walk in them… (Hosea 14:9)."*

Perhaps Elijah felt like a certain twelve year old boy did who was trapped into a hard life of digging shale from broken coal. A kind, caring man saw the lad weary of life and filled with despair and asked him, "Son, do you know God?" Quickly and with little emotion the boy replied, "No. He must work in some other mine." He didn't deny the existence of God, but he did know that God did not work there.

People who have seen the downside of owning their own business in network marketing because of company failure, lack of knowledge, skills, guidance, misdirection, poor products/services or their own lack of effort may well conclude that God is still God, but He does not work in network marketing. As a result, they shy away from it like the bubonic plague. The critics of network marketing may seem to be everywhere. This is merely a result of simple numbers. There are more people capable and willing to invest small start up and maintenance amounts in home based businesses than there are people capable and willing to step out and invest one-hundred thousand dollars in a franchise, or open their own retail store. If you talk to a thousand people who have seriously researched, invested and applied themselves in the network marketing industry and one-thousand that have opened their own conventional businesses you may find similar rates of satisfaction. But because of the shear volume of people who have ventured into the industry, you may hear that God cannot, must not and does not work in and through network marketing.

They put God in a box of their own making. They inadvertently put limitations on God's wisdom, restrict His Omniscience, shackle His Omnipotence and void His Omnipresence.

God is bigger than men and woman who place the importance of capital over character, income over integrity and greed over goodness. He is bigger than the trickling brook. He's there to give Elijah and you guidance and security in the worst of times. He has neither disappeared or departed or distanced himself.

Where was God when Elijah's brook dried up? He was still on the throne and in perfect control. This is a constant reminder that God is not controlled by circumstance but is in control of circumstance. He can make the business of network marketing a miracle for your life and future. Don't allow men to put manacles on the Miracle Worker. God has not gone out of business even if your brook has dried up. He is still God. **He is still merciful and He can turn your disappointments into peace, contentment and joy.** It all starts here and at times in unfamiliar ways.

The man caught stranded in a flood didn't comprehend the possibility that his rescue might come from a different source than what he had expected. First of all the police showed up and offered to give him a ride, which he refused. A short time later as the water continued to rise, a boat was close enough to get him to safety, but he would not crawl on board. As the situation worsened, he crawled on top of the roof and was soon spotted by a helicopter, which made an effort to lift him from the rooftop, and again he refused to cooperate.

Tragically he drowned, and as the story goes, appeared before God only to ask God why He didn't save him from such a tragic death. God's reply was, "I tried. I sent you a squad car, a boat and a helicopter." God did His part, but the man failed to see his opportunity.

Unfortunately, **we limit God** by **failing to see God working through unusual circumstances.** Take a look at the possibilities that God could be offering you through network marketing.

- The ability to work from home
- An alternative or additional source of income
- Work flexibility – You can work in the am/pm, any day of the week, in person, on the phone, on the internet
- The opportunity to own your own business and be your own boss
- Low risk, cost contained start up and operational expenses

- The opportunity to become a part of a team of likeminded individuals who help each other succeed
- A supportive environment with mentoring and training
- Tax advantages of self-employment including business expense deductions
- Local, national and in many cases international markets
- They are in general and in a few cases, no risk

One brook may have dried up in your life, but God is ready, willing and able to replace it with an ocean of His abundant supply. Charles J. Rolls expresses some characteristics of God beautifully in these poetic words. "We know assuredly that His vitality never varies, His fervor never flags, His agility never ages, His fortitude never fails, His feet never falter, His will never wavers, His dominion never declines, His constancy never changes."

We do not depend on brooks. We depend on God! Seek His direction.

Chapter 3

Scam or Scarecrows

Scarecrows are lifeless, harmless distractions designed for the singular purpose of keeping animals and birds from enjoying the fruits of a harvest.

Scam is a nasty, four letter word along with the words scheme and pyramid that are frequently but incorrectly used synonymously with network marketing. These words infer that individuals have been raped financially, and that intentional deception has taken place. Unfortunately, it is a slap in the face and an embarrassment to hard working, sincere, honest network marketers. Society at large would agree that scammers should be rounded up and thrown into a slammer and the key thrown away, but honest people working to make a living should be respected, not degraded for their search and work to achieve the American Dream.

As in most industries there are crooked and dishonest individuals. These scammers are scarecrows that are simply lifeless, harmless distractions designed for the singular purpose of keeping you from reaping an abundant harvest. They are not the essence or fair representation of what network marketing is and can do for you. A Christian business man Thomas L. Haines and his neighbor, L.W. Yaggy put network marketing in true perspective when they said, "The first step toward greatness is to be honest, says the proverb. But the proverb fails to state the case strong enough. Honesty is not only the first step toward greatness, it is greatness itself…in the long run, character is better than capital."

Elijah was not a scam artist using trickery and emotional sabotage to take advantage of a woman who didn't have a nickel to her name (I Kings 17). You might question his methods but not his character. He was following the Lord's direction. He just happened to be presenting an unconventional method for meeting a severe crisis. The widow may have had doubts with his unorthodox proposal, but the plan he laid out was in fact her families' salvation, providing her with a daily supply. Initially, Elijah may have looked crazy, but when she applied his guidance the end results were miraculous. He did not take advantage of her. He gave her an opportunity to take advantage of God's economic stimulus plan, and it worked.

As in every industry, honesty depends on the individual in the business, not the business itself. As Christians, we make decisions every day in our lives and in the business world as to whether we strive to be like Christ. Some fail, some succeed. When making your business decision, look at the individual, not the 'bad press.'

These quotes appeared in the *Fort Worth Star-Telegram* April 26, 2009. The bold headline was: "Riches or rip-off? A regulatory agency calls it the "phantom riches tactic." It goes on to remind us of a $65 billion Ponzi scam that unraveled. Scammers are the scum of the earth, but they must not become scarecrows that drive us away from legitimate opportunities.

Alexander Pope fine-tuned the value of honesty when he wrote; "An honest man is the noblest work of God." Network marketing is not the problem. Misdirected or dishonest individuals have given the industry a black eye, but those of integrity can change the bad reputation by adopting and following this motto.

I will
- Be authentic
- Treat people fairly
- Be honest
- Practice unwavering integrity
- Avoid proliferating misinformation and disinformation
- Cling to and promote family values
- Help the poor, needy, fatherless and widows
- Celebrate what others can become by God's grace
- Be a good steward in every area of my life

- Be an encourager
- Set an example of good work ethics
- Develop a passion for the economic opportunity, service or product I represent

Shakespeare may have said it about as well as it can be said. "This above all: to thine own self be true, and it must follow, as the night the day, thou canst not then be false to any man."

The Good Book takes this issue to a personal and practical level as well. Jesus said, *"And as you would that men should do to you, do you also to them likewise."* (Luke 6:31)

Chapter 4

The fastest way to fail is to fail to try.

"Only those who dare to fail greatly can ever achieve greatly." – Robert F. Kennedy

Matthew 25:25 in the parable of the talents the rebuked man said *"And I was afraid, and went away and hid your talent in the ground;"* (The Open Bible New American Standard).

Playing it safe may be the most dangerous thing you can do in a climate of economic recession or depression. After a few hard years of farming, one fearful and doubtful farmer thought he had stumbled onto the right solution. Instead of stepping out again, he decided to play it safe and not even plant a seed. This man had the land, the time, the knowledge and seed, but he didn't have the nerve to try again. A stranger happened by one day and seeing the field untilled and unplanted asked the dirt farmer if he was going to plant some cotton. "No," the farmer replied, "I'm afraid that boll weevils will destroy the crop and all my profit with it." "How about corn?" the stranger continued. "No way, they are predicting a long dry spell and no rain. Corn won't grow in that climate. It would only swivel up and die before harvest." The stranger was confused with the answers he had received and posed one final one. "Are you planting anything at all?" "Not on your life," he said, "I'm just playing it safe." **Obviously the result of fear and lack of action is lack of harvest.**

The surest, fastest way to fail is to fail to try. The triumphs of those who tried are recorded in Psalms 126:5-6.

> *"And now, God, do it again—-bring rains to our drought-stricken lives so those who planted their crops in despair will shout hurrahs at the harvest. So those who went off with heavy hearts will come home laughing, with armloads of blessing."* (The Message).

Notice that *"they planted their crops in despair..."* It was both a tough time and a time for trust. The tougher the economic climate becomes the greater must be our trust in God. I try to stand on Proverbs 3:5-6 every day of my life. It says, "Trust in the Lord with all thine heart; and lean not unto thine own understanding. In all thy ways acknowledge him, and he shall direct thy paths."

These tough times of layoffs, cut backs and moratoriums raises the awareness of our need for guidance from on high. A Lewis Harris Poll found ninety-six percent of Americans lay awake at night concerned about two things: health and finances. We can't afford to make mistakes. One step in the wrong direction can be disastrous to our happiness and security. The widow woman in I Kings 17 had to have felt the hot breath of hunger, poverty, fear, depression, and anxiety breathing down her neck when she met Elijah. At that moment she couldn't afford to make any miscalculations. She only had a small portion left. Elijah proposed that she pitch in her last reserve of corn meal and cooking oil, and then give him a portion.

It was a scary risk, but what did she have to lose? Now be sure of this. The surest and fastest way for her to fail was to fail to try. She tried and her needs were met beyond what she could have imagined because she was walking in God's direction. **Her prayers were answered after she stepped forward out of her fears.**

Try. That's the key. Try something. You will never know whether you will succeed or fail unless you try. Network marketing may be a scary thought to you, but you will never know how dynamic and life changing it can be until you try.

Follow the advice of Winston Churchill. He said, *"Success is never final; failure is never fatal; it is the courage to continue that counts."*

In 1902, the poetry editor of *The Atlantic Monthly* sent a sheaf of poems back to a twenty-eight year old aspiring poet with this curt note: "Our magazine has no room for your vigorous verse." The poet that tried and eventually succeeded was Robert Frost.

Albert Einstein was a man who was not afraid to try. In 1905, the University of Bern turned down his Ph.D. dissertation as being irrelevant and fanciful.

Thomas Edison spent two million dollars on an invention that proved to be a flop. He never failed to try and the world is a better place to live as a result of his efforts.

There you have it. The surest, fastest way to fail is to fail to try. Don't let that be your epitaph.

Look for a solid network marketing opportunity and a supportive mentor and do it. I recognize that it can be like searching for a needle in a hay stack so I would like to offer you a few suggestions to follow as you make that tedious task of finding a company and seeking out a mentor that will invest in your efforts.

When looking for a viable network marketing opportunity your prayers should be consistent with Solomon's. He did not ask for wealth, prosperity, or kingdoms. He asked for wisdom to lead the Lord's people and the Lord blessed him with much more than he asked. **Begin with sincere prayer for wisdom in your search and if there is anything in your life not right between you and God, start by asking for forgiveness and praying for guidance and discernment. He will not forsake you or leave you, and he will guide you and give you wisdom.**

Look inside before looking outside.

Before choosing a company, begin with an honest evaluation of yourself and what you are willing and able to invest from a time, monetary and personal effort and also where your interests lie. This is so important because as Christians we are called to not only believe in Christ, but to serve Him. Our walk means as much or more than our talk. It is no different with a network marketing business, successful network marketers believe in their opportunity, service or product and it is so much a part of our lives that people who know us know we are Christians AND what we do. We are not ashamed of the Gospel of Christ, and we are not ashamed of our network marketing business. This level of belief pours out of us into others, inspires others and promotes loyalty.

Sometimes, as Christians, we fail to live up to our calling and sometimes, as networkers, we fail to represent our opportunity with resounding success, but staying the course is what leads to the harvest.

This is where many novice networkers falter because they join a company and never establish their belief system. Christians without boldness have difficulty sharing their faith, just as individuals with doubts or embarrassment are unlikely to succeed in the network marketing industry even if they are with companies where others are succeeding. Just as with the gospel our responsibility is to plant the seed, we can't make someone else believe; we just provide an opportunity to the best of our ability.

Develop your faith
New Christians need development of their faith. New networkers need development of their knowl-

edge and skills. Choosing a sponsor or leader that will provide you with support in the learning curve is critical. As important as it is for a new Christian to establish themselves with a solid Christ centered Bible teaching church family it is just as important for a networker to establish themselves with a team that will support and mentor them in their building of their network marketing business. Ask about support, training systems, and the success and experience of the individuals who will directly sponsor, support and train you. <u>Given will power enough, brains enough, and faith enough, almost anything can be done.</u>

Choose the right company

Now, let's talk about the importance of choosing the right company. The doomed passengers that boarded the Titanic on its maiden voyage did not do anything to cause the ship to sink, nor were they able to change what was to happen. They just boarded the wrong ship. Joining a network marketing company for certain is not life threatening. <u>However, your investment and hard work can sink if you join the wrong company.</u>

Let the buyer beware is a motto to live by. Take time to research the network marketing companies that you are interested in. Do your homework before you take the plunge. The following general guidelines will be valuable in screening the good from the bad.

1. Take your time. Don't allow anyone to rush you. A good opportunity to build a business

in a multilevel structure will not disappear overnight.

2. Ask questions concerning:
   - The company history and its officers
   - The products – their cost, fair market value, source of supply and potential market in your area
   - Required initial and monthly purchases
   - Any company guarantees
   - Average earning of active distributors.
3. Read the company literature.
4. Consult with others who have had experience with the company and its products or services.
5. Be sure that there are actual products or services being sold. Pyramid schemes are built on 'money for nothing.' Cash is exchanged, but there is no legitimate product or service.

Portions of this list were compiled from published information by the *Direct Selling Education Foundation,* a Washington, D.C. not-for-profit public education organization. It is tax-exempt and contributions to it are tax-deductible. The objective of the Foundation is to serve the public interest with education, information and research, thereby encouraging greater public awareness and acceptance of direct selling in the marketplace.

You want a company with solid finances. A ground floor or start up company with less than three million in available resources may undergo challenges in establishing itself in the market and be limited in its ability to sustain growth. A three to five year old company continuing to demonstrate growth or a company older than five years with consistent sales typically has the financials to support their compensation payouts throughout ups and downs. Each of these three company positions has pros and cons.

The general definition of a ground floor opportunity is that it has not reached one hundred million a year in annual sales. **Ground floor opportunities** have significant potential for growth and there is plenty of room for first time networkers to make significant incomes. Research is critical into the management and financial backing of these companies. When evaluating a ground floor opportunity look for a product or service that has mass market appeal, the financial capital to survive the first two years when a majority of new companies fail, a strong management team and a compensation plan that returns your investment quickly. Ground floor opportunities have potential for great reward, but also entail the greatest risk. Because of the high risk of failure in the first two years, be prepared to work to achieve your initial return on investment and be aware that you may be looking for another company soon; keeping in mind if the company succeeds the payoff from the beginning growth cycle of a company can be immense.

Now let's look at a three to five year old company. These companies have demonstrated the ability to survive the first two years, so now you need to evaluate the sales and potential for growth. What is the momentum level in the company? Are they continuing to grow and expand? These companies have a lot of promise for providing solid opportunity for the entrepreneur with lower risk, but look for momentum potential or your paychecks may not see the benefits.

And finally, consideration of **companies older than five years** must entail research into their current situation. Are they continuing to grow? Do they have a visionary management team that is keeping them in the current trends? Are they updating? Are their leaders still excited and does the compensation plan pay the novice distributor?

The companies to avoid are those that are new and lack stability or those that are older and stagnant in their growth and momentum. Finding a company you can be on fire about with solid finances and momentum growth is the perfect frame for your success regardless of the age of the company.

Regardless of the company you choose, to avoid the negatives of the industry literally calculate what it will take for you to receive your return on investment. This one factor can keep you in the industry, motivated, excited and working. Realistically some people don't pick the right company the first time. It's like going to the movies. You can see five movies that you thought were going to be great. One you may wish you had stayed at home instead of watching, three were good and one was excellent and you tell everyone about it. The critical factors in choosing the company for you are: can you be passionate about it and do you have someone who will mentor you in the business?

A product and service analysis

Look closely at the products or services. The key words in choosing the right product or service are **PROPRIETARY, CONSUMABLE, AND RENEWABLE.** Proprietary means you cannot get it anywhere else other than from that company. Consumable and renewable means that the product or service is used regularly and individuals are likely to sign up for a monthly order on a long-term basis. These words mean that there is the necessary foundation for the compensation plan to pay immediate and residual income. There also should be a unique quality, something that sets it apart from others on the market, and which appeals to a large base of consumers. Companies which have products or services that make a difference in people's lives are also preferable because they instill loyalty even when the users are presented with an alternative or when they are making monthly budget decisions.

The compensation plan

Unless you have been in the industry, evaluating a compensation plan may be difficult. It's like reading the most detailed part of any business. Here are the top questions I recommend:

- What is the initial investment?
- How many people do I need to receive my initial investment back?

- What is the monthly requirement to receive a check?
- How many people do I need to get my product/service free monthly?
- What is the quickest way to build my business in this compensation plan i.e. 2x2, 4x4, wide, deep? And who will walk me through this?
- Look for a company that provides as much in their compensation plan as it does in their product or service. Sometimes a compensation plan can be one of the best products of a company.

Choosing a sponsor, mentor, business partner

First let me say, that many individuals are introduced to a network marketing company by a friend, family member or acquaintance. In this situation you may be blessed to have someone who you know that will be a strong mentor to you, but in other cases your sponsor may also be in a learning curve, so you both may need to look upward in the sponsorship line to find a strong, experienced mentor willing to invest in your training and business growth. If you don't have an active sponsor, then call the company and ask them whom they would recommend. In seeking long term support look for someone in the sponsorship line above you who will benefit financially in the pay plan from assisting you and has the qualities described in the passages to follow.

In the scenario, where you are searching for a company and a mentor, don't allow the scam artist to scare you away from what can be a legitimate and abundant harvest!

Let part of your research include choosing whom you will work with. Open a new revenue stream, but do so discriminately. Don't sow among thorns. Thorns not only choke out good seed and prevent a good harvest, but they can also hurt people. There are many that have ventured into the network marketing field, tripped over rocks, been pricked by thorns or fallen into holes.

That's a major problem in venturing out into this arena without an honest mentor. As in any chosen field, taking the right initial step is an important part of reaching the abundant harvest that lies ahead. How can a person choose which one to pursue without getting hurt by thorns of inexperience, unrealistic hype or disingenuous salesmen? A mentor or leader can help you make the right choices in this journey. They can turn your weaknesses into strengths, obstacles into stepping-stones, and disaster into triumph. Choose a leader you can be confident in and willing to follow. Look for someone

- *Knowledgeable* about the product/service and business. You will know this in the first few times you talk. Look for someone who is complete and concise, not who over talks each detail.
- *Accessible* on a regular basis to assist you in learning, recruiting and training. This is easily identified by "How can I reach you?" "When

are you available?" "If I join how often will we communicate in the first ninety days?"

- _With teaching skills_ that is willing and able to provide you with feedback that will help you develop your own skills. Ask to listen to a recruiting call this person does with another person. You learn a lot from these in regards to experience, ego and skill.
- _With honesty and integrity._ If they say they have been successful in the business, leaders in companies are typically listed in the company newsletters, highlights, etc... Talk to people they have worked with. Talk to people they have helped. Pray for spiritual discernment and seek honesty and integrity in their communications.

Experience is a desirable quality in a leader. If they have built an organization, made significant income, communicate well and are willing to spend time teaching you then you will benefit from their direction. Then be willing yourself to take the direction and feedback they provide.

So we have covered a lot of what to look for to reduce risks, now let's talk about risks. Consider John Steuri, a division general manager of IBM who had a philosophy that is worthy of our consideration when weighing risks versus rewards. He said, "Talk about the importance of taking risks. We've got to be more entrepreneurial. Nobody is taking risks; they are all playing it safe. Playing it safe is dangerous."

Peter had to step out of the boat before he became a part of a storybook miracle. Moses had to listen to a burning bush. Noah had to build a boat for a hundred years with no clouds in the sky. The risk is always on our part — not God's. God is always faithful to do what He said He will do. **…AND IN FAITH…** The next move is yours.

If you are new to the industry or have tried and failed keep this powerful challenge William Durant threw out in mind. He said, **"Forget past mistakes. Forget failures. Forget everything except what you're going to do now and do it."** You will never succeed unless you try.

Chapter 5

Hope not Hype

"In the factory we make cosmetics, but in my stores we sell hope." - Charles Reason

Efforts to communicate at times are about as unsuccessful as trying to communicate with a signpost. Let's clear up one misconception. Talking is not necessarily communication. In reality, communication has not taken place until the person to whom I speak hears not only what I say but understands what I mean!

Robert Browning, a famous British poet, published *Sordello* in 1840. Baffled readers resorted to the poet for an explanation of some statements that were made in this particular writing. Browning read through it twice, frowned, and then shrugged his shoulders. "When I wrote that, God and I knew what it meant, but now God alone knows." I've been to some network marketing meetings and left with the same sensation. There were all sorts of hype, but when it was all said and done and the lights went out, what were they talking about? Honestly, I wondered if God even understood.

Understanding and conveying what network marketing and direct sales means to the ordinary person is critical to our success. We must be certain that we understand what we are talking about so that the hope, potential and real part-time, full-time career opportunities are not lost in words, hype and unfulfilled commitments.

The popularity of direct sales and network marketing

Direct Sales has an estimated fifteen million people involved in the U.S, and more than sixty-two million worldwide. Most of these are women, though nearly a third are men or two person teams such as couples.

The real time and money making opportunity

The Direct Selling Association lists the median annual income for direct selling distributors in the United States as twenty-five hundred dollars a year, or just more than two hundred a month. Approximately ninety percent operate their business part-time. Less than eight percent of distributors put in forty hours per week or more. Of those working full-time, twenty-five percent earn more than a hundred thousand annually.

The new multilevel marketing is career based and does not require stocking or 'garage certification'

Multilevel marketing is a popular way of retailing in which consumer products are sold, not in stores by sales clerks, but by word of mouth. Independent businessmen and women work where, when and how they choose. They can work anywhere that they can make contacts, in person, on the phone, by mail, on the internet, etc. Many companies refer to their salesman and women as distributors, but the industry has evolved and few companies still require the individual to stock and distribute products or services.

Career description of a network marketer

In every field there are descriptions of the responsibilities and the work and pay schedule. A network marketer is an independent business owner working for a company paid to make contacts with other people, complete follow up with the contacts, and then mentor interested individuals to repeat this process. This can be done on a part-time or full-time basis and done consistently can produce immediate and residual income, as well as bonuses.

In a multilevel structure you can also build and manage your own sales force by recruiting, motivating, and training others to share those products. Your compensation then includes a percentage of the sales of your entire sales group as well as earnings on your own sales to retail customers. This opportunity has made multilevel marketing an attractive way of starting a business with comparatively little money.

The Market (Hope or Hype)

This venue is becoming increasingly interesting to people who are struggling to make ends meet. The Fort Worth Star Telegram on April 29, 2009, announced that General Motors would close up to twelve hundred dealerships and lay off thousands of workers.

The same edition published a report that temp agencies have taken a huge hit losing twenty-seven percent of their jobs in the past year according to the Bureau of Labor Statistics.

A long time friend of mine went in for a conventional job interview recently. The interview began after general formalities with a series of questions, which were aimed at discovering his Care levels. The purpose of these questions was to discover what meant the most to him and made him tick.

The questions were pre-designed for reflections and response. The interviewer asked, "How much do you care about the car I drive, the house(s) I own or the money I make?"

It was not what he had expected, but without hesitation my friend replied, "None." Perhaps in half jest and half sincerity the interviewer blurted out, "That's what I thought. You are hired." Then he fired off the next and possibly the most important question. "Why?" The candidate for employment responded, "Nothing you have matters to me, because it adds nothing to my net worth, annual income or will help me to achieve the American Dream. You see, I see this job opportunity as a bridge to a brighter tomorrow for me, my family and our personal hopes."

That's the bottom line. At the end of the day, the passion of your own heart, prayerfully directed, is the best compass you have to follow. **One of life's greatest tragedies is not that you did not reach your goals, but that you had no goals to reach**.

<u>Find a need and fulfill that need.</u>

What draws many to the industry and what turns many away is what is perceived as the hype associated with the industry including the portrayal of expensive cars, fabulous mansions and million dollar incomes. This is typical of sales and recruitments in most industries. Remember the line "Show Me the Money!" It is the selling of the success stories. We also see it in weight loss where we see those who change from significantly overweight to bikini and muscle bodies. We see it in educational markets where children change from despising school to thriving on it. Success sells and we all know it.

Don't let this hold you back or turn you off when you hear the "hype", rather let yourself put it in your "if God gives me a miracle" place. Network marketing has produced millionaires, so when you are turned off by the presentation keep in your mind "what if…" and also look at them realistically reading the small print that says, "this is not representative of the average person." Let hype, not only be the sales portion, but hope and motivation, it could happen for you.

Modify hype with realism. Most people beginning in this industry today are looking for day to day income, ways to supplement current income, ways to pay the bills and are then eternally hopeful of hitting it big along the way. For those of us working this as a business where we truly desire to help others and meet their needs we have to look at each person's situation, desires, skills and needs. We are all made different. Our needs are different. Our goals are different. Perhaps if an opportunity that fits my needs and expectations were presented to me it may just be what the doctor ordered.

There are many in need, who need God more than they need an opportunity, but who may be reached with the good news through a legitimate opportunity. God not only knows our needs but has promised to provide for them. Philippians 4:19 declares, *"My God will meet all your needs according to His glorious riches in Christ Jesus."* God is a need fulfiller and millions in the world need to know it.

There are 13.6 million single parents in the United States alone out of which 27.7% of those are mothers living on Poverty Street with their children. Entering the job market for a single parent is complicated to say the least. It means getting childcare, updating their wardrobe, transportation expense, etc. The list goes on and on and all this from an already cramped budget. Network marketing is an ideal, realistic option for many of these single parents.

Retirees whose nest eggs have vanished need to hear this message of hope. Working from their home is far less threatening than going back to the conventional work force and searching for a job. At their age, it would be like looking for a needle in a haystack.

In these difficult economic times, your friend, your neighbor, the person in the grocery line, your boss, everyone you meet may need the opportunity that network marketing provides.

Even churches and charitable institutional income budgets have plummeted. The Northwood Church's income in Keller, Texas has. Pastor Roberts said, "They've got all the resurrection they want. This church is scrambling to meet parishioners' secular problems as well as spiritual needs."

The Richland Hills United Methodist Church in Richland, Texas will be offering a seminar for job seekers twice each month.

First Methodist Church in Fort Worth, Texas is sensing a need to do something to help members of their congregation in these desperate times and will be coaching people on how to give prospective employers a 10-second "evaluation speech" about themselves.

A recent survey of National Association of Church Business Administration members found that 32% said their church has financial difficulties. This percentage has rocketed by 14% in 2009 alone.

The church has an obligation as well as a privilege to minister to the basic physical and financial needs as well as the spiritual needs of their congregation. We can offer hope, hype and reality income. We just need to know how, when and where to offer what we have.

Looking to the market

Advertisers are jumping on board because they can see the handwriting on the wall for much of what we call conventional business. "By 2011, companies are expected to spend $26 Billion on internet classifieds." This is the projection reported by Jupiter Research, 2006. They are moving the way the buying trends are moving, and tooling out their market strategy accordingly. If we are to be successful we must not allow the market to move away from us slowly but surely. We must go after the market.

Look at advertising. 50% discounts on furniture. 10 items on the lunch menu for less than $5. Buy a car and if you lose your job we will make the payments for 12 months. Buy one and get one free. Don't be naive. This is not a benevolent, charitable obsession that is taking industries by storm. It is an adjustment to the market trend and needs.

I'm not suggesting that we sponsor a network marketing garage sale in the basement of corporate headquarters. But I am proposing that we become more creative and user friendly when we present our products, services and opportunities. Simplicity is often perfection in communication.

Examine the thought provoking inquiry that A. Whitney Griswold made. *"Could Hamlet have been written by a committee, or the Mona Lisa painted by a club? Could the New Testament have been composed as a conference report? Creative ideas do not spring from groups. They spring from individuals. The divine spark leaps."* We need the divine spark to fire our imagination and inspire creativity. Where there is a will there is a way. We must do something different. It may be inconvenient and even revolutionary, but why does it matter if it is a passageway to success?

Look at the market you are approaching squarely in the face. Most of them are not superstars likely to knock the ball out of the park or guru's that will be looking to stuff millions into their pockets. They are people who need another $500 a month in their monthly budget. This is not greed. It is need. Marian Wright Edelman summed it up nicely when she said; "It is time for greatness, not for greed." And I might add – there is enough money in the network marketing industry to supply everyone's need that chooses to participate and create.

Follow this simple rule:
- Find out what people need
- Fulfill that need

Hype panders to greed. Hope addresses needs.

We would be wise to assume a posture of offering hope and dropping the hype in favor of fine-tuning our product/services to address the actual needs that people have, not what we assume they need. Look at the buying trends through their eyes not ours.

Those of us who choose network marketing and direct sales as a career need to change "the star of the show". We need to not only advertise and celebrate the big splashers of the industry, but also honor and celebrate the "little guys" who took a chance on a network marketing business and had their dream come true. There are many more of these who don't make the magazines but who have had their monthly budgets supplemented. **Through a part-time home based business their dream for adding an extra $500 a month was achieved. Success should be judged as return of investment and positive cash flow for a business.**

Jesus certainly reversed the trend in His day. He didn't come to be top dog and have people washing his feet. He washed feet. He didn't come to be served but to serve.

Where the industry has failed in their marketing is selling the great expectations and missing the boat of demonstrating how many can achieve realistic expectations for solid part-time income. Too many have quit because they haven't 'won the lottery', but would have succeeded beyond part-time incomes if they had just kept consistently working what they had.

The comparisons are easily made to Christian witnessing. If you are told, come with me to church, believe and all of a sudden God will make all your troubles go away and every day will be wonderful, then you are shooting for unrealistic expectations, but if you know that becoming a Christian will produce trials and tribulations with a greater reward in Heaven, then you will stay with it day in and day out, committed to Christ.

If you are told, come join my company, talk to people and you can become a millionaire quickly with little to no work, then you have been sold a bill of goods or you are naïve. If you rather see this as a solid investment in a product/service and an opportunity that is going to take making contacts, following up and teaching others to duplicate your efforts, and you realize this will take time and effort repeated over and over, then you are seeing the big picture of an amazing industry and you have the correct expectations that will allow you to stay with it day in and day out, committed to achieving the income you desire.

Chapter 6

The Silver Tongue

I Corinthians 13 "If I speak with human eloquence and angelic ecstasy but don't love, I'm nothing but the creaking of a rusty gate..."

Kindness has influenced more people than eloquence.

Listening is an art that network marketers and direct sales people have not mastered. We are taught to talk, and we do an excellent job at that. But we may be talking to people about things they don't necessarily want to hear. They may not want to know about mansions, Mercedes and millions, company assets, product or the company compensation plan *until they know that we care about them and are able to provide them with a business that can provide them with the basics in a reasonable amount of time.*

Elijah put his heart into his presentation, and left the decision to the woman. He trusted God's direction and her judgment. This is a point in network marketing where some begin to resemble and mimic the Federal Bureaucracy who does not believe that Mr. and Mrs. John Q. Public have the ability to weigh facts and make their own decisions wisely.

Present what you honestly believe can help someone through your product, service or opportunity and put some heart and genuine caring into the mix. I Corinthians leads us into charity, caring and loving.

Love:
- doesn't strut,
- doesn't have a swelled head,
- doesn't force itself on others,
- isn't always "me first,"
- doesn't fly off the handle,
- doesn't keep score of the sins of others,
- doesn't revel when others grovel,
- takes pleasure in the flowering of truth,
- puts up with anything,
- trusts God always,
- always looks for the best,
- never looks back, and
- keeps going to the end.

In the passage of Scripture in I Kings 17, the penniless, single mother was at the end of her rope and Elijah found that out very quickly. Listening to her revealed so much about who she was, what she needed and where she was in life. Once he knew that, he could proceed with a plan custom designed for her. He didn't try to validate his credentials or outline his previous accomplishments. He just showed up and made her an offer she could not refuse. He knew what she needed by listening and gave her a workable, practical solution. It was a win/win situation.

Who got the best deal? Not Elijah. He got one meal out of the deal plus any handouts she gave him. She got an abundant supply. It was her meal barrel and oil can that never ran out. It was hers to do with as she pleased. Face the fact. If the woman had not seen the benefit for her and her son, then all the talking, outside validation and pressure would not have changed her mind. Can you see the difference? Opportunities that fit a person's need don't have to be sold just told!

Realistic goals are reasonable and attainable! Return on investment, monthly covered products and services and positive cash flow are the beginning steps in an industry with limitless income potential. Begin with helping those that have a need.

This will be a better world when the power of love replaces the love of power. "Love never fails."

Chapter 7

The Something for Nothing Lie

"The men who try to do something and fail are infinitely better than those who try nothing and succeed." - Lloyd Jones

Nothing plus nothing still equals nothing

When you get something for nothing, you usually get an abundance of what you paid for, NOTHING! And yet, it is one of the biggest, most effective lies that the public accepts as gospel truth.

Anyone who has been in church for any length of time has heard two passages of scripture that are frequently quoted to give comfort and hope, but to many people they actually become constant reminders of unfairness caused by misinterpretations perpetuated by well meaning people who do not know what they are talking about. Jude refers to such people as "clouds without rain" and fruit trees that whither and die without ever producing fruit (Jude 12). Expectations without realization equal disappointments.

The first passage is referred to as a parable in which Jesus teaches a timeless, true to life lesson on sowing and reaping. (Matthew 13:3-9) In that passage we discover three undeniable, universal laws that contain a roadmap to prosperity. The three components are the Sower, the Seed and the Soil. As is the case in most parables, it brings heavenly truths down to earthly terms.

The second passage is found in the book of Galatians where Paul, the apostle, states "whatsoever a man sows he shall also reap, IF HE FAINT NOT." (Galatians 6:7-9) Once again we are confronted with an undeniable, universal law.

Relevancy Realized

If these passages of Scripture have no relevancy for our day, then they have no more value than if we were hosting a Lamaze class to expectant parents in a geriatrics ward at the hospital. However, the verses are not journalistic efforts made to market the agricultural industry.

The Magnificent Man from Galilee was embedding a timeless business success strategy in simple terminology. Someone once observed that a teacher can take a simple truth and make it complicated, but a communicator can take a complicated truth and make it simple. Jesus made it simple. This is a synopsis of his success strategy made simple.

- **Individual initiative** is a key component. The story begins by telling us that a "sower went forth..." He was not punching a clock on a regular 9 to 5 routine. No supervisor was going to call him or write him up for being late for work. He had self-discipline to push himself to the limits. You must have it if you want to succeed.

- Secondly, he was driven by a **singleness of purpose**. The Bible explains that he went forth "to sow." He had one job to do and was not confused for one moment about what he could and would be doing consistently.

- In the third place, he had **unquestionable confidence** in the seed he was planting. He knew what he was doing was going to produce an abundant harvest.

- In the fourth place, he had an **undefeatable attitude**. Some fell in places that defied all of his efforts, but he kept right on sowing knowing that the next seed he sowed might well fall on productive ground.

- In the fifth place, he understood the necessity of the **need to make an initial investment**. Seed costs something, and he did not expect something for nothing. He invested in the seed without which there would be no harvest.

- And finally, he visualized and accepted that **what he was doing was a process**. It was not an overnight, instant gratification windfall. Seed requires time to grow. Unless you understand that you will faint and fail to reap your reward.

This is the essence of the Universal Law that will never be amended or rescinded.

The Universal Law

First, let me explain the meaning and significance of a **Universal Law**. The term is simply defined as a rule of conduct or action recognized as binding and enforced by a controlling authority without limit, prejudice, or exception. Carefully, re-read that term and definition again and again and commit it to memory. It can arguably be one of the most important lessons you will ever learn.

Universal laws are over arching principles that govern the plight of the universe and all its inhabitants. They are not restricted to any gender, age or race. The Universal Law of sower, seed, and soil is the true combination out of which reproduction and harvests are produced. The Universal Law of whatsoever a man sows that shall he also reap is not complete within itself. Paul adds a critical aspect to the principle, which is a condition, *"if you faint not."* You see the Universal Law covers the sower, the seed and the soil, but the negotiable principle remains. It involves my volition, determination and perseverance. I must not faint or give up or someone else will reap my harvest.

Fainting feelings are especially prevalent during emotionally stressful times, financial crisis and job searches. It means to become weak and timid and things become indistinct and unclear. Consequently, decisions are difficult to make. T. Boone Pickens, the wealthy and extremely successful businessman makes this provocative statement about indecision and timidity. "Be willing to make decisions. That's the most important quality in a good leader. Don't fall victim to what I call the ready-aim-aim-aim-aim syndrome. You must be willing to fire." That is one of the purposes of this book. We want to provide you with enough information, motivation and Biblical principles so that you can and will make quality decisions in every area of your life including those decisions related to network marketing.

A decision making model

POOR DECISIONS ARE OFTEN THE RESULT OF HAVING POOR INFORMATION. HISTORY WILL SUPPORT THIS PROPOSITION 100%. Follow the telephone wire all the way back to the first one ever produced. With the information that we have today about the invaluable contribution that the telephone has on the world, we would expect that the citizens of the world stood on tip toes and applauded the decision to make such an instrument. Such was not the case.

A man who was marketing this strange apparatus in New York was arrested and charged with attempting to extort funds from ignorant people who saw possibilities in this device which he said would convey the human voice any distance over metallic wires so that someone on the other end of the tiny wire could actually hear the voice of the other. That poor man was hooted off the streets and thrown into the slammer all because people jumped to bad conclusions for lack of sufficient information.

Most new ideas are doomed to a similar fate, and network marketing is included in this mix. Unfortunately, the public is not getting the truth, the whole truth and nothing but the truth. As a result, bitter bias and premeditated prejudice makes it near to impossible to make honest decisions about network marketing in the present unfriendly environment.

It's time for old-fashioned gumption. Stand on your own two feet. Speak for yourself. Don't be a Polly Parrot repeating what others have influenced you to say. Make your own decisions. Refuse to be an intellectual piece of milk toast and bow to the pressure of blind public opinion. New ideas such as network marketing are not always popular, and popular ideas are not always right.

Demand your intellectual freedom and make your own decisions. You can do it. It's as easy as A, B, C.

> **A.** Arrange for an honest, thorough examination of the facts.
> **B.** Break away from the public perception pressure and do a personal "mind sweep" to clear your head of any degree of bigotry.

C. Consider all of your options carefully.

D. Distinguish the difference between facts and fiction.

E. Seek counsel from experienced, wise, trustworthy people.

F. Factor the ultimate value of prayer into your decision making process.

G. Goad yourself in demanding mental freedom to make your own decisions.

Making decisions is as simple as A, B, C, and the better the decisions you make, the bigger your paycheck will be!

Smaller pay checks means bigger challenges and sleepless nights. How many times in your life have you asked yourself the question, "why do bad people seem to do so well, and here I am as a confessing believer having more month on my hands than I have money?" I truly believe that the people who import and integrate the Universal Law of sower, seed and soil into their lives, regardless of their church affiliation or belief system, are rewarded with the fruits of their labors, "if they faint not." It is the UNIVERSAL law and will not fail now or ever.

For example, the law of gravity is a universal law and is just as applicable to the wise as the unwise, and the pervert as well as the pure. If either jumps out of a window on the 10th floor, they will both go in the same direction and suffer the same fate. The universal law works for one and all at all times and in all places.

We have a tendency to forget that God sends rain on the just and the unjust (Matthew 5:45). **He gives opportunities to everyone, and the ones who have seed in the ground and not in the barn will benefit from it.** It's the universal law.

MANY in the Christian community have HAD OPPORTUNITIES KNOCK AT THEIR DOOR AND FLATLY IGNORED THEM. We can agree with Mark Twain who declared that "I was seldom able to see an opportunity until it had ceased to be one."

The disciples saw opportunities for success in their vocation as being months away, and were blind to present potentials that were all around them. Procrastination paralyzed the entrepreneurial spirit, but Jesus said, "Say you not four months, and then comes harvest. Behold I say unto you, lift up your eyes and look on the fields; for they are white already to harvest (John 4:35)."

On another occasion He made this strange statement. "Having eyes to see, you see not (Mark 8:18)." These people were suffering from entrepreneurial blindness. They couldn't see the watermelon for the seed, the banana for the peeling or roses for the thorns.

The side effects of this blindness are too numerous to count, but there are four that are predictable. They are paranoia, envy, cynicism and criticism.

- **Paranoia** is an assumption that everyone is against them and that they are being persecuted without cause. Success is impossible for them to achieve because everyone and everything is against them. They are blind and cannot see.

- **Envy** is the desire for something that someone else has that you feel you deserve and should have instead of them.
- **Cynicism** is one who resorts to sarcasms and even ridicule without regard to the harm that may be done to the person who is the object of their wrath.
- **Criticism** is fault finding whether expressed openly, behind closed doors or even in whispers.

Voluntary blindness to this degree is proof positive that it is easier to criticize than to be creative. Don't fight new ideas. Small minds are the first to criticize great ideas and the last to embrace them.

An old Proverb leads you to a good place to change directions for your life and pull the blinders from your eyes. It says:

Count your blessings, not your crosses,
Count your gains, not your losses.
Count your joys instead of your woes,
Count your friends instead of your foes.
Count your health, not your wealth.

Entrepreneurial blindness need not be final or fatal. I pray that your eyes will be opened to see that it is a grave error to believe that you can get something for nothing in the world of business and specifically so in network marketing. "Whatsoever you sow you will also reap if you faint not…." It's the universal law, and it will work profitably for you.

With success at stake, let's examine the 3 critical ingredients of this Universal Law, that when combined, produces a harvest; and put them to work for us in our lives.

The Sower

The *sower* is defined as: "a person who sets something in motion or begins an enterprise." Wow! This is where it can start for you. A seed cannot be planted and remain in the bag at the same time. Begin to think of something you want to set into motion and head for a predetermined, desirable destination. Begin an enterprise. Start a home business. Release your entrepreneurial spirit and God given potential.

Elijah, in I Kings 17, set something into motion that an economic downturn, pessimism, criticism and fatalism could not slow down or stop. It was an unstoppable, undeniable, uncomplicated plan of God. He dared to sow a seed of hope and economic stimulus into the life of a single parent who had next to nothing, who had to step out in faith, who was about to lose her son and yet whose faith was richly rewarded. Elijah sowed a seed, and God provided a harvest.

When we pray for the will of God in our lives, we also must believe that He has given us spiritual gifts and spiritual seed to achieve that which He has promised. Our God is an awesome God. He watches over the sparrow. He clothes the fields with flowers, and we are His children. You may not believe in Him, but He believes in you!

Take the first step. No one can do this better than you. You have the ideas and passion, but you must begin. Listen and learn what Dwight D. Eisenhower taught. He proposed that *"We succeed only as we identify in life, or in war, or in anything else, a single overriding objective, and make all other considerations bend to that one objective."* All great ideas and unfilled hopes can usually be traced back to a mental set back or a reluctance to take that first tiny step. A lifetime of regret usually follows when we look back on what might have been.

Don't spend the rest of your life wasting time wishing you had made better choices. Make a commitment now. "Commitment unlocks the doors of imagination, allows vision, and gives us the right stuff to turn our dreams into reality." - James Womack

Dream busters must be dealt with if you are to succeed. They will try to convince you that you are not cut out for your type of dream. Or you may be so beat up and disappointed that you do not have the energy to hope against hope that all things are possible for you. But let me remind you that this is consistent with Satan's view of you and contrary to your Lord's perspective of you, His child. He looked upon creation and said, "It is good."

The fact is that there are those who have confounded the world by overcoming the odds and on their 10th, 50th, 100th attempt, unruffled by countless failures, driven by passion they have crossed the finish line as winners. Vince Lombardi, the legendary football coach was absolutely correct when he said, "Winners never quit, and quitters never win." Don't quit sowing. The more you sow the more you reap. If you are not willing to be a sower, one who initiates a forward motion, then your noble goals can never become a reality.

Stop and think. What enterprise, what home based business would you launch were it not for limits, fears, insecurities, failures and voluminous negative influences? What is the "it" factor that you have always desired but have put off, and maybe have not ever shared with one solitary soul?

Congratulations! This is the time and place to begin. You see the beginning of the harvest is the sower who will begin an enterprise, set into motion hopes and dreams, and trust God to be God. Take the words of Kay Lyons seriously and apply them to your life today. She said, "Yesterday is a canceled check; tomorrow is a promissory note; today is the only cash you have—so spend it wisely."

I can assure you that the Universal law is not limited by your fears and failures. Don't allow the failures of yesterday or the fears of tomorrow to prevent you from starting something that by the help of Almighty God you will finish. For without sowers, there will be no harvest.

The Seed

Now that a person has made a decision to set a plan into motion, what comes next? The second ingredient that is indispensable for a harvest is the *seed*. A seed is defined as: "An embryo capable of normal germination resulting in a new plant." IT IS CAPABLE, but only capable to germinate when properly planted. The seed within itself is not enough to produce a harvest. It is only beneficial when the sower places it into the ground and sets the harvest potential into motion. Then and only then is the miracle of God capable of taking place.

The seed, in this case, is the God given embryo that you possess. It is your stamped DNA. It is His spiritual gift to you and unique only to you. It is the mind of God that has been carefully and creatively placed inside of your brain. The Bible explains it in these awesome words. *"But we have the mind of Christ* (I Corinthians 2:16).*"* How incredible to grasp what that means to you as an independent business person. Simply put, it means that a molecule of the mind of the Creator has been placed in your head, a piece of the Mind that made all matter. All that matters is inside you and is capable of doing great things.

This reminds me of a story concerning the daughter of Caesar. A friend of Julia, Caesar's daughter, tried to persuade her to abandon her extravagant life-style and live more in accordance with her father's simple tastes. Julia refused with this brief explanation. *"He sometimes forgets that he is Caesar, but I always remember that I am Caesar's daughter."* That is the crux of the matter. We must never forget who we are, and that we are more than a piece of dirt with a set of lungs. WE HAVE THE MIND OF CHRIST. GOD IS IN US. God forgive us of our moderation and small-mindedness.

We are called to be mighty men and women. Will Rogers is reputed to have said, *"The trouble with our financial giants was that they did not giant."* You have a seed planted in you by your Maker that can become a giant in the network marketing business or any other business, but you must see it, believe it, act upon it, commit to it and persist in it.

Norman Vincent Peal wrote these words in *The Woman's Home Companion:* **"Millions of men and women are creeping through life on their hands and knees—merely because they refuse to rely on any power but themselves."** Get a grip! Release your God given potential. It is IN you. Let it go.

Further more if you are unwilling to invest your seed then once again you are deceived and will eventually suffer defeat. Remember the phrase there is no free lunch? It's absolutely true. *You are believing a lie if you think you can get something for nothing.*

Already I can hear snickering voices saying, "Ah, ha, salvation is free through grace, not of our works." Yes, it is true but don't confuse free to us as meaning without cost. The cost for our salvation required a great seed invested by the Heavenly Father into the earth and that great seed was Jesus.

Let's all do ourselves a favor and never confuse free as meaning lack of investment. In our search for survival and financial stability, some vigorously resist the slightest possibility that they should be required to make any investment in a home based business. They, for some unknown reason, assume that they should be able to get something for nothing.

I talk with people on a regular basis that run from any suggestion that investing in a legitimate business opportunity is appropriate and logical. I am not a CPA, but simple math teaches me that nothing plus nothing equals nothing.

Folks, no seed - no harvest. It's that simple. Debate over. The foundation of legitimate network marketing is that a company pays individuals for word of mouth advertising and the consistent purchase of products or services to fund a percentage of base pay out. If there is no embryo planted into the ground, then you are fooling yourself no matter how you spin it or whom you blame it on. **Your creative thoughts, the levels of energy that you are willing to invest, your money, your commitment, all will determine the potential you have as seed.** And remember this. A seed reproduces after its own kind. You cannot sow seeds of one kind and expect a different kind of harvest. If you are expecting a certain harvest, you better be prepared to sow the seed you are looking to eventually pick and eat. A sower who is unwilling to invest seed is expecting something for nothing and will get nothing but disappointment in return.

The Soil

The final ingredient is the soil. For clear communication, let's work with this definition. *Soil* is the medium in which something (seed) takes hold and develops. The Bible is clear on this subject. Not just any old soil (medium) will work effectively. You cannot plant your seed in an asphalt jungle and expect to reap a fantastic harvest or any harvest at all. Logic teaches us that the planned harvest will fail due to the inability of the asphalt to take hold of the seed and develop it for a harvest. This does not mean the asphalt is not good for other purposes, but it is not capable of developing plants and producing a harvest.

Any farmer will tell you that the soil (medium) has to be proper for the life of the seed to reach its potential. Other surfaces serve different purposes but seeds require depth to develop root systems to grow and produce. It is no wonder that people armed with good intentions have set out to sow and failed to produce little if any harvest and concluded that the UNIVERSAL LAW had failed miserably. No. The Universal Law did not and will not fail. The truth is the good seed fell on bad ground.

The problem wasn't the sower, the seed or even the law. It was the lousy soil into which the seed was planted. Again, no matter how willing the sower may be, how potent the content of the seed, if the soil will not or cannot support development, all your dreams will be squashed.

This applies to network marketing and direct sales dramatically. We have all seen good seed — good intentions, good work ethics, good business plans, and good goals — planted with companies promising something for nothing and ran head first into a brick wall. The pain and disappointments are tragic. So they end up throwing the baby out with the wash. Good news! This is not the end of the world. It could be the beginning of a great tomorrow if you can realize that the problem is not the sower or the seed. It is the soil. Richard Bach's insight is incredibly accurate. He said, "What the caterpillar calls the end of the world, the master calls a butterfly." Don't be a caterpillar. Be a master and release the butterfly within you to fly. It's time to let her rip!

It is a glaring mistake to assume for one moment that all networking marketing opportunities have the same soil (compensation plans, company financial stability, record of success, etc). Examine the soil for its richness and proven ability to develop the seeds of others before you dive in.

Network marketing businesses just like any other business (soil) must be evaluated for their compatibility with your beliefs, its marketability, consumability, profitability and potential for longevity. The seed in unfertile soil yields no more harvest than, no seed in fertile soil! Do your sowing carefully the first time, and you will have no regrets at harvest time.

"He that goeth forth and weepeth, bearing precious seed, shall doubtless come again with rejoicing, bringing his sheaves with him." - Psalms 126:5

So remember, no seed, no harvest, no joy. You will never get something for nothing, and keep in mind; you miss 100% of the shots you never take. Take a shot at success and win the prize!

Chapter 8

On your mark. Get set. STOP? No, evaluate, and then accelerate!

"The will to succeed is important, but what's even more important is the will to prepare."
- Bobby Knight, Former Indiana University basketball coach

"Gentlemen, start your engines" is the signal that the Indianapolis 500 race is about to begin. Fired up fans are on their feet, hands waving in the air as the sound of massive, fine tuned engines send out a deafening roar. The cars circle the tracks, and then the green flag drops and the race is on. The next 500 miles is a carefully planned journey jockeying for position to win the race. Pit stops, tire changes and positioning were all spelled out on paper long before the race began. They stopped to prepare before they were set to go.

Most of us feel pressure to succeed in much the same way, and admit it or not, we feel we are being judged by others in most, if not all areas of our lives. It's not as obvious as the winners and losers of the Indianapolis 500, but we are judged by the car we drive, the clothes we wear, the house we live in, the clubs in which we hold membership and the tombstones that tower over us after we are dead.

Unfortunately, most of this judgment is heaped upon us based upon the size of our paycheck. We are not just breadwinners. We are competing for acceptability in our society at large. That's one reason why we spend countless hours preparing and worrying about *the next hurdle* in life hoping that it will in some way validate our existence to our peers. This can be an exhausting continuum of frustration and deep despair until we finally realize that it is a losing cause. In this state of confusion, we can doubt our self worth and feel like a nobody when God has made us a somebody!

Dr. William Glasser studied human nature and behavior and concluded that:

"All psychological problems, from the slightest neurosis to the deepest psychosis, are merely symptoms of the frustration the fundamental need for a sense of personal worth. Self-esteem is the basic element in the health of any human personality."

God wanted you to know that you are somebody special and inspired these words in Psalms 139:14. It reads like this. *"Thank you for making me so wonderfully complex! It is amazing to think about. Your workmanship is marvelous—-and how well I know it."*

Paul encouraged you to recognize who you are and your great worth as a person when he wrote. **"We should not live like cringing, fearful slaves, but we should behave like God's very own children, adopted into the bosom of his family, and calling to Him, Father, Father (Romans 8:15)."**

This constitutes the first step in the process of self-evaluation and is a winding journey that requires honest introspection. You must also have confidence in knowing who you are and how that affects your life pursuits. This must have been the way the widow women examined her life as we reflect on the story in I Kings 17. You see, she did not need a mind altering, prophetic revelation to jar her into the reality that she was down to her last meal. Nor did she need a gentle angelic nudge from heaven to snap her back into "the real world" and humiliate her with the bare fact that she was unable to provide the basic, daily necessities of her precious son. Necessity drove her to explore possibilities that she had never encountered before. Survival instincts paved the way for experimentation in unfamiliar territory. She may have encountered a vision of something she had never had before. Jonathan Swift described vision as "the art of seeing the invisible." Opportunity and hope are invisible, but she saw them.

She saw the opportunity and seized it in hopes of giving her and her son a better life. As a matter of fact, it was an opportunity to seize life itself. I wonder how many of the men who lost 2.4 million jobs in the United States in the past few years might see network marketing as an opportunity to discover a better life or just an opportunity to make a mere living for themselves and their families. In either case, network marketing for some offers hope in hopeless conditions.

Could it be that of the 1,596,270,108 (that is billions) of the world internet users many may have turned to network marketing and direct sales as a means of finding income streams that had dried up elsewhere? I do not know the answer to that, but I do know from statistics that internet usage worldwide increased by 342.2 percent from 2000 to 2008 and that online retailers are acquiring new customers at a 15% annual rate versus 2% for traditional brick and mortar retail outlets. (Deloitte & Touche USA, 2006)

With jobs drying up in the conventional employment circles, the internet is an exploding opportunity, but you must see it to realize the potential. Recall, "Vision is the art of seeing the invisible."

The destitute widow in I Kings 17 must have "seen the invisible". Although she was caught in the traffic jam of economic failure, she still somehow, someway was motivated to offer what she had to the man of God and hope for a brighter tomorrow. This was more a statement about who she was and less about what she had. Her gift came from within not from without. She was teachable and willing to do something different in order to reap different results.

So what do I mean by EVALUATE, AND THEN ACCELERATE! Before you push the pedal to the metal and accelerate you must take time to evaluate so you do not end up getting ready, getting set and then STOPPING.

For just a brief moment, take your foot off the pedal on the right side of the floor board and slam the one just to the left to the floor, come to a complete stop and do not pass go! In our sleep, we know how to go, but in many cases, we never even give consideration to where we are going, how we are going and who will be going with us. I love what Laurence J. Peter had to say about this subject. He said, "If you don't know where you are going, you will probably end up somewhere else." Stop before you start and make sure your first step is in the right direction.

Any other action is a form of insanity. You will finally arrive somewhere at a neck breaking speed but be sorely disappointed and frustrated that this is not where you wanted to be.

Going faster is not always the best and safest way to go. Passengers on an ill-fated flight discovered this when they heard the pilot's voice making an announcement over the intercom. *"Ladies and gentlemen,"* he began, *"I have some good news and some bad news. The bad news is we have lost one engine and our direction finder. The good news is we have a tail wind, and wherever we are going, we are getting there at the rate of two-hundred miles per hour."*

93

Don't lose your direction finder. It is the key to ultimate success for network marketers. Never fly by the seat of your pants. Make your plans and work your plans. Evaluate before you accelerate.

In the business world, the direction finder is referred to as a business plan and is essential to the ongoing evaluation process. I have found these questions to be the foundations of a successful investment, marketing and growth business plan. I hope they will assist you in accelerating swiftly and accurately.

1. What is my initial financial investment and monthly investment requirement?
2. Who is supporting me in this plan? How experienced are they? What is their availability?
3. What are my strengths? (Am I a good communicator? Do I have computer or internet skills? Am I good at marketing? Am I good at closing a sale?)
4. What are my weaknesses? (Do I have limited contacts? Am I afraid to talk to people? Am I afraid of rejection?)
5. What kind of people should I be marketing to?
6. Who are the people I plan to market to first? Friends, family, people in my community, people I don't know who I get from advertising?
7. How will I contact these people? In person, on the phone, on the internet, by mail, through classified ads?

8. How many hours per week will I invest in my business?
9. How many people will I contact per week?
10. What are the tools I need?
11. What are the things I should say?
12. What must I do to receive my initial investment back?
13. What must I do to achieve $500 a month?
14. What is my plan when someone says they are not interested?
15. What is my plan when someone says they are interested?

Evaluation Process

The word *evaluation* means to determine the significance and worth by careful appraisal and study. Elijah was a great evaluator. The same can be said of the widow woman. Each of them had a reality check. The "now" was fresh in their minds and they did not attempt to ignore or avoid the facts and rush on to the next level of living. He knew his brook had dried up and she knew she was destitute. Facing the "now" honestly and forthrightly will prepare you for the future. Procrastination was not a viable option for Elijah or the widow. There was no time to put off making decisions for another day. This was not a time for concern. It was a crisis and they reacted accordingly. Elijah called for a decision on the spot. No dilly dallying and procrastination was allowed.

The question is how about you and me? Are we like driftwood in a rushing stream going wherever the water takes us and at the speed it chooses? Or are we deliberately charting our course, making our own decisions and setting our own pace? Evaluation is critical. Only those who are able and willing to innovate and adapt to consumer trends and new opportunities will survive. Many job markets are drying up, look at the growing trends that are riding out the economic tide.

Wayne Gretzky, one of the greatest hockey players of all times, had a philosophy for succeeding in hockey that should become a part of the play book for network marketers. He explained his strategy for playing the game with these simple words. *"I skate to where the puck is going to be, not where it has been."*

Sadly, most people are going where business has been, not where it is going. More and more, however, people are turning to where business is going and one of the trends is business that can be done on the internet with the world as the market place and in many network marketing venues a low start up cost. Delottie & Touche USA, 2006 reported that U.S. consumers were expected to increase their retail online spending from $877 per consumer in 2005 to $1,512 per consumer in 2009.

Stunning as it is, 14% of *INC., 2002* magazine's 500 fastest growing companies in the United States started with less than $1,000. This is an evaluation process and conclusion that opens the door to thought. "Go where the puck is going to be, not where it has been."

Our hopes of a better lifestyle are far too often exploited by a play on the emotional fear factor and ill-conceived marketing ideas that became fiascos. As a result, the average American picks up the pieces of his/her fondest dreams and finds him/herself back at ground zero to nurse his/her wounds and shattered emotions. Are our emotions important? Absolutely, and without question. Polly Adler was correct to write, "The heart often knows things before your mind does." One guy had the heart of passion printed on a bumper sticker, which read: "Passion Rules." It ruled Joe Montana, who was MVP of the Super Bowl, two different times. His teammate, Ronnie Lott, described the passion that Montana had in this dramatic statement. "You can't measure the size of his heart with a tape measure or stopwatch."

Emotions are critical, but decisions must not be made on emotions alone. Hype and subjectivity must not cancel the value of evaluation.

Many businesses, large and small, conventional and non-conventional have succeeded as well as many have failed. Many individuals regardless of talents, skills, nationality or other attributes have succeeded as well as many have failed. Many churches, Christians and pastors have ministered well and many have failed miserably. Network marketing is no different, but often times it is judged differently. If twenty children drop out of school, does that mean school is bad? If twenty children leave home, does that mean parents are bad? No! One thousand times no. It only means that each individual situation should be carefully evaluated on its on merits and the network marketing industry is the same. William

James was 100% correct when he gave us this advice. "The art of being wise is the art of knowing what to overlook."

We must learn to overlook the element of human error, the voices of bitter critics, the cost of engaging in a potentially profitable business and the constant presence of fear.

Ruth Fishel made it perfectly clear that "courage is fear that has said its prayers." We should not overlook the power of prayer when engaging in the evaluation process.

The evaluation process should begin with me. It's not the company or the product or the service or financial stability of the corporation. These are vital and absolutely necessary. But is must start with me. What do I want? What do I need? What does my family need? What do I believe can and will happen if I give it my best shot by the help of God? What company, product or service am I most comfortable with? How much time am I willing and able to give to this venture? How much can I afford to invest? To overlook this component would be a huge mistake!

In reality, we have all had victories of one sort or another. We have thank you notes, trophies and results as proof, but we cannot survive on past victories. As a matter of fact, they can distort our picture of reality.

One of the most difficult things for a person to do who has been laid off, out right fired or demoted at the office is to realize that past victories are not a consolation prize in crisis situations. They will not pay the bills or keep a roof over your head. For some, it means biting the bullet, swallowing pride and doing what needs to be done without the consent or approval of your peers. This then could mean searching for help and hope in a new and different direction. Perhaps at that point, network marketing may become more of a solution than a problem.

Acceleration

Now let's talk about acceleration. The word, for our purpose, means the rate of change of velocity with respect to time. Interesting. Velocity and time fit like a hand and glove. You may want change but have refused changing your pace or method. Have you ever said, I need to change but now is not the time? Will Garcia rang the bell for change loud and clear. He reminded us that "the first step toward change is acceptance...change is not something you do, it's something you allow."

These are powerful words coming from Melvin B. Tolson.

> **"Since we live in a changing universe, why do men oppose change?... If a rock is in the way, the root of a tree will change its direction. The dumbest animals try to adapt themselves to changing conditions. Even a rat will change its tactics to get a piece of cheese."**

The big question is not do we need change. We know we must change or we are through. The question then is how committed are we to change?

Change requires change. It's that simple. I have heard that insanity is defined as continuing to do the same thing, the same way, over and over and expecting to get different results.

Change is breaking old habits and following a new road map, but make sure you have the right map that will guide you to where you want to go. A pastor friend of mine was driving to Dallas to do a wedding, but he did not know how to go where the wedding was being held. The groom sent him a road map, and he followed it to the "t" and it led him to a dead end street with no wedding hall and no delicious bride's cake. I know what you are thinking, but I think you are wrong. You are surmising that the groom sent him to the wrong address to get out of making a commitment. Well, you are wrong or at least I think you are. The fact is that the map company had not updated their maps and he followed the map to the end of the world as far as that map had it drawn up. He just had the wrong map.

The map was his evaluation point, and he was accelerating as fast as the law would allow; but only getting to the wrong place in record time.

You must first determine where you want to go, and then choose how to get there. Remember, you can walk, ride, or fly, but this will only determine how quickly you will get there. Evaluate and chart your course, then accelerate to get where you need to go as fast as you can.

This is the general philosophy of network marketing. You choose where, when and how to begin your drive for success and how quickly you want to get there. All of these choices are yours, and two additional big plus factors are that you can work from home and have a successful networker as your mentor.

The Master Teacher summed up what we might refer to as: On your mark. Get set. STOP. He said, *"Is there anyone here who, planning to build a new house, doesn't first sit down and figure the cost so you'll know if you can complete it? If you only get the foundation laid and then run out of money, you're going to look pretty foolish. Everyone passing by will poke fun at you: He started something he couldn't finish* (The Message - Luke 14:28-30)."

Evaluate the situation. Count the cost. Commit to the plan and claim the prize!

Chapter 9

The Boogie Man Strikes Again
(Once you accelerate, watch out for the speed bumps)

"When a man is defeated by life it is always due, ultimately, to the fact that he is suffering from (a) spirit of fear...The spirit of fear is the real, the ultimate cause of all failure in life, and of all unhappiness."
– Dr. Martyn Lloyd-Jones

T he most frightening part of my day when I was growing up was bedtime. When the lights went off my imagination came alive. My closet became a dark cave with a bottomless pit of ghosts, and the lamp on my dresser was transformed into a mean monster that had a special dislike for children. All of this was enough to cause the hair to stand up on the back of my neck, but it was that ugly looking Boogie Man hiding under my bed in the daytime and prowling at night that kept me from making a run for it.

I could almost feel him grabbing my leg, pulling me screaming and kicking under the bed to make me his midnight snack. My only hope was to pull my shield, which happened to be my cotton bed sheet, over my head and wait for dawn. It was a hopeless situation until I remembered the light switch on the wall. If I could reach the light switch, the mysteries of the darkness would all be gone. Then in one last ditched effort, I lunged for the door and turned the light on. Schazzam! The light sent the Boogie Man back where he came from.

The Bible says, "Fear has torment..." (I John 4:18), and no one knows that better than the business man or woman struggling with the Boogie Man lurking in the shadows trying to steal their dreams. All of us would agree with William Shakespeare who wrote: "Of all base passions, fear is most accursed."

Bertrand Russell summed it up well in this simple statement. "To conquer fear is the beginning of wisdom."

I can almost hear you saying, "Great, but how can I do that?" "How can I overcome the fears I have?" The answer: one prayer, one step, one day, one fear at a time. Our Lord knew we would have fears. There are 365 passages in the Bible on fear and there is obviously a reason for that. Without fears, without trials, without tribulations, we do not learn to lean on Him. We do not depend fully on Him. We do not grow and we do not mature.

The fears you will face in your business are minute compared to the fears you may face in life, but do not discount the power of those fears if you give into them, but take heart, we have the ability to overcome.

There are practical ways to grow out of our fears, just as we grew out of fear of the Boogie Man under the bed. Let me walk you through some steps that will help you to get beyond your fears and achieve what God has designed for you.

<u>First of all realize that transformation begins with *identifying the source of your fears so you can face them.*</u>

You must know specifically what your fears are and where they are coming from before you can understand them and take steps to overcome them. From years of experience in the industry I have observed fear of disrespect, rejection and failure.

One of the first fears that goes through people's minds when they enter a network marketing business are: "What will my friends and family think?" People don't know what to say when someone laughs or ridicules and says "I can't believe you joined one of those scams." They cringe at the idea of telling someone about their business, product or service and seeing, hearing and feeling the rejection of a family member, personal friend or even a total stranger. The feeling of rejection hurts no matter where it comes from. For the building of your faith, realize that Jesus was tempted in all ways, ridiculed by many, suffered the consequences and arose victorious. Rejection can be crippling or strengthening. Then, of course, there is the fear of failure, of putting your financial resources, especially in this economic environment, into a business where loss can be experienced.

Now, that I've said all of this out loud let me walk you through how you can face your fears, meet them head on and achieve success. Great news! You do not have to face your fears alone.

Keep in mind, you didn't just wake up one night and the Boogie Man was gone. It may have been your mother, father, brother or cousin taking your hand to look under the bed and then leaving the night-light on for you that gave you the confidence to close your eyes. Maybe it was just the light down the hall leading to your parent's room that gave you the courage to run to the bed or maybe it was just maturing beyond the idea of a monster under the bed.

Begin by aligning yourself with a company, product or service that you can truly believe in and with a team of individuals who will support you in this endeavor.

This search is critical for your success. For some this comes easily, for many who have failed before, the search is much more difficult.

Next to spreading the gospel and loving others, service, encouragement, and edification are certainly Christian principles that work hand in hand with network marketing. The industry is built upon the premise that one person helps the next. You may have heard Sponsor, Train, and Teach to Sponsor,

Train and Teach. A good sponsor in the business can shine the light that makes the Boogie Man melt away. People in networking circles typically believe in the person recruiting them, before they believe in or buy the product or service. You are not fighting the Boogie Man alone. You have a team holding your hand and showing you the way and as a Christian you have a God that will never let you down no matter what you face.

Secondly, *take immediate action to dispel your fears.*

Fear does not dissipate or completely go away without a fight. It will require radical action to get maximum results. I suggest that you follow this rule. What you can do, you ought to do, and what you ought to do, by the help of God, do. You must put forth the effort, and God will furnish the grit to do it effectively. Trust your faith and doubt your fears. Do this by developing a sincere enthusiasm for the product or service you have to offer.

John Madden, a Super Bowl winning coach maintains that the difference between the guys who make the Pro Bowl and those who don't is enthusiasm. A nation wide cross-industry study found that the most significant factor that distinguished the "top" from the "good" sales performers was enthusiasm.

In a unique book titled, *If it ain't broke... break it,* the gifted author quoted a top executive headhunter in explaining what he looked for in his search for leaders.

"The thing that makes the difference between a good manager and an inspiring, dynamic leader goes beyond competence. It's passion. That is the single quality that is going to lift a person head and shoulders above the rest in these tough times."

Get some fire in your belly as they say in the sports world. It will help burn out your fears. You now know you are not alone and you have a company, product, service and opportunity that you can stand behind with integrity.

Look at things from a different vantage point.

Looking through someone else's eyes can change perspective dramatically. Look through the eyes of those who have succeeded in the industry. Network marketing has created part-time, full-time, and million dollar incomes. Even well known millionaires have recently demonstrated their belief that this industry provides opportunities for anyone and everyone regardless of the economy and in many cases in spite of the economy.

Look through the eyes of your customers. Network marketing companies as with other industries are generally founded on fulfilling the needs of individuals through products or services or financial opportunities. You have something people need. In 2000, The Direct Sales Association reported 55% of Americans have purchased goods or services through direct sales.

The industry is not a scam or a pyramid, there is money exchanged for a product or service. **The company pays you to advertise, it is as simple as that and it offers you the amazing opportunity to invest what is a small start up fee, work from home, network and make income. So, realistically assess the opportunity and put your fears behind you.**

Lastly, discipline yourself to *take on only one battle at a time, track your success and have fun.*
You won't win every battle, but you will give each challenge your full attention and effort. The Bible warns us to avoid being "double minded" which might be defined as out of focus. James 1:5-8 paints a great picture for us to study. It says, "If you don't know what you're doing, pray to the Father. He loves to help. You'll get His help, and He won't belittle you, when you ask for it. Scripture says to come boldly before the throne, in the will of God to ask as children before a loving father. Ask boldly, believingly, without a second thought (The Message)." These verses assure us that God wants to help. Don't have a second thought.

Keep a scorecard of your successes and reward yourself accordingly. You will win some and lose some, but keep score on how many more wins you have than defeats. Reward yourself in victories. Treat yourself to a banana split and rebuke the calories in advance. Tell someone so that they can rejoice with you. The splendor of success can lose its luster if you have no one to share it with.

I have great admiration and thanks to Vivien Yeiser Laramore who penned this note for all of us to remember. *"I've shut the door on yesterday and thrown the key away—Tomorrow holds no fears for me, since I have found today."*

Look not back with regret, nor forward with fear. Thank God for today and fears will slowly go away. Remember, that God modeled for us hard work and rest. Some people don't know how to rest or have fun or don't let themselves. They fight for survival, fume over situations they cannot control, and forfeit the opportunity to love and be loved.

Aaron Burr had it figured out correctly. He said, *"The rule of my life is to make business a pleasure and pleasure my business."* Believe it or not, conducting an honest, profitable business can be fun as well as work. I have found this to be true in network marketing because I choose the people with whom I work and can develop camaraderie. My work mates can become my best friends and confidants.

In many ways they bring I Corinthians 12:24-26 to me in living color. It says,

> *"For no matter how significant you are, it is only because of what you are a part of... the way God designed our bodies is a model for understanding our lives together as a church: every part dependent on every other part, the parts we mention and the parts we don't, the parts we see and the parts we don't. If one part hurts, every other part is involved in the hurt, and in the healing. If one part flourishes,*

every other part enters into the exuberance
(The Message)."

Sometimes you can get past a fear, by not looking
at it. If you don't look under the bed, but just at the
covers then you will move faster into the bed. It's all
about staying focused on the goal. If you can't see
the Promised Land, the struggles between here and
there can be overwhelming and far less than worth-
while. Network marketing and direct sales profes-
sionals must maintain a Promised Land Mentality.
We must see the end from the beginning and never
lose sight of the prize.

An obstacle is what we see when we take our
eyes off the goal. Never, ever forget that the prize is
worth the price we must pay to succeed, and there are
no bargain basement discounts.

Elijah was far, far from a Boogie Man. He was
in fact God's Blessing in disguise. When the widow
first caught a glimpse of him, he looked like anything
but a blessing. The desert sun, often reaching 120
degrees in the heat of the day, had burned his skin
brown. It looked like a piece of swiveled up leather.
His face and chin were covered with hairy months of
growth, and the dusty, sweaty mantle that was draped
around his body was not a photo that would grace the
next cover of GQ magazine.

**The fact is that God sends blessings our way
in packages that don't seem to fit the opportunity.
We look for God to do it one way, and He chooses
to do it another. Look for blessings in unlikely
places, and you may well find them there.**

Say this out loud "The Boogie Man will strike again, but I will be ready. I'm headed for the Promised Land, and he can't stop me." Quit staggering around in darkness. Turn the light on and the opportunities will look bigger and the Boogie Man will fade out of sight.

Chapter 10

The one size fits all lie

The size of your success is determined by the size of your belief.

Football buddies are life-long buddies. We have moaned together, groaned together and grown together. I look back at an old manuscript and marvel at the wisdom it teaches me. It says, *"A faithful friend is a strong defense: and he that hath found such a one has found a treasure."*

I had and have such a friend. Let me tell you a little bit about him. As he grew up he always had a consistent problem of finding clothes to fit him. And as you know, there is nothing more uncomfortable than wearing a garment you paid hard earned cash for, getting it home, trying it on and finding it so tight that you were hardly able to breathe.

We have all had shoes that squeezed the blood out of our feet, shirts that did not accommodate our newfound growth spurts, or pants that refused to allow relief when we sat down to relax without having to unbutton them. Thanks be to God who gives us relief through spandex and elastic.

Believe me when I say, ONE SIZE DOES NOT FIT ALL. To say and believe otherwise is a bald faced lie. He has been the poster child for special order fits forever. It was a common occurrence for him to have a permanent mark tattooed on his forehead due to the wrong size helmet or baseball cap, which was forcefully placed on his dome. Finally, his battle with life-long headaches was traced back to the source. His big pumpkin head never found comfort wearing things that seemed to fit everyone but him. Clearly after trying every fix or remedy nothing changed. He was destined to suffer when he was required to wear a hat. After observing him, I can tell you with all honesty and candor once again that ONE SIZE DOES NOT FIT ALL.

Many of you can relate to this fact in other areas of life. Your head size might not be the problem, but you have issues that have forced you into the rank and file of the un-fit -able. Listen, my colleague had no choice in the size of the watermelon he toted around between his shoulders.

Some of you have had no choice in some of the cards you were dealt but have had to deal with the fall out. At the time of this writing my football buddy has battled for thirty-three years with a major crisis that to this day he has difficulty knowing how to handle. His family was, by most standards, what you could call a normal home of a very prominent and well-respected Pastor. Even with that statement, this big tight end on the football team was forced into a preacher kid category, which in many ways is a non-fitting situation. He never knew if he would fit in as the new kid in the youth group, a new school or just simply the new kid on the block and a preacher's kid at that. All he could do was trust the God that had called his Dad into the ministry to work everything out.

As shallow as it may sound, living with the concerns of the annual board meeting in some ways gave him the heebie-jeebies as he waited anxiously for them to validate his Dad's ministry by vote. This never set well with him then and still does not to this day. The very thought of it makes his skin crawl.

With that being said, let me leave no doubt in your mind that that was the lifestyle, which his family agreed to and were honestly proud to accept the good with the bad. In hindsight, he admits that he is grateful for the experience and will be eternally thankful for the toughness of his Dad and his unwavering commitment to push him and his sister to greatness regardless of their circumstances. Not to fill your head with the assumption that he is pointing a finger at anyone, allow me to simply point out that another individual made one single choice over which his father had no control but for which his father would be held accountable. Their lives quickly left the realm of tranquility and moved without delay into the vortex of a tornado that left them holding on for dear life. Here is where the story gets really intriguing and inspiring.

You see, this choice of someone else to pursue another path placed my friend and his family in a state of shock and disbelief, for the first time, they were introduced to the world of the un-fit and began to understand what Phillip Yancey calls "un-grace." No matter what anyone verbalized they were seen differently. Their lives were put under the microscope of unfair criticism without merit. His dad's life-long ministry/career was called into question without the slightest care or concern about the truth. Truly they were cast into a wander land without the first clue of how or why or knowing how to get out.

Without apology, I can tell you that you really find out how many true friends you have when you are fighting for your sanity and dignity. My teammate says that he can understand why you fear no evil, because the path is deserted. You become marked, considered dangerous to some, feeling not for your pain but fearing potential losses or guilt through association. II Corinthians 4:8-9 says *"We are* troubled on every side, yet not distressed; *we are* perplexed, but not in despair; Persecuted, but not forsaken; cast down, but not destroyed;" Our mutual hope is that you will not allow your lonely journey to be a catalyst to prove the nay sayers correct as he did. Choosing retribution or retaliation will only make bad matters worse. Be not distressed, despaired, forsaken, or destroyed instead opt for forgiveness and perseverance. He understood what J. Harold Smith meant when he declared, "Never does a man stand so tall as when he foregoes revenge, and dares to forgive an injury."

Ruth Bell Graham, wife of the world famous evangelist Billy Graham, said, "Every cat knows some things need to be buried." A buried past is the beginning of a bright future.

The people around you may have you tagged as a "bad egg", but don't believe it. The only voice that really matters is the one inside of your heart. Listen for the Holy Spirits still small voice. Whatever has made you "not fit" in the eyes of some of your contemporaries is no reason to believe that God does not believe in you. Let me conclude by saying that over the years many of those nay sayers have rallied around my buddy and his family maybe realizing their mistakes or just simply proud of the perception that their family has rebounded victoriously. Whatever the case they have moved on, and you must do the same.

My reason for sharing this story **is to encourage you to remember that your situation and feelings are no longer an excuse to throw up your hands and quit. You have got to rebound and put yourself back in the game.** It amazes me as I read the story of Elijah that God directed him to the widow women as a replacement resource for his dried up brook. It doesn't take a great thinker to realize how improbable that show of intervention really was. Get the picture, Elijah had been on easy street with provision without worry or fret for some time. All of a sudden the brook dries up and no more ravens were delivering three meals a day to his doorstep.

At this point most of us would have clamored about why is this happening to me? Am I out of the will of God? Is there sin in my life along with count-less sleepless nights? Not Elijah. *It was a simple indicator that the place of provision had changed not the provider of the provision.* You see this is where we lose focus. God has different plans for us but His promises stay the same. He will still provide. With that being said God did not consult Elijah on where he should go for his next meal, didn't garner Elijah's vote of confidence, he simply said go to Zerapath and there you will find what you are looking for.

Little did Elijah know that his provision, not provider would be found in a widow woman who was broke beyond broke and literally down to her last meal. Not only that but out of the mouth of the place of provision she said my son and I will eat this last meal and die. Without negotiation or restraint Elijah says, "Put out an extra plate and feed me as well. Oh by the way if you do, you will never have to worry about food again." At this point you may be asking why in the world would God allow the prophet to go to a one meal women and take food from her mouth. *What we overlook is her last meal became the begin-ning of her endless supply of food forever. You see sometimes what we think is our last bread invested in the right place births the forever.*

We all are guilty of profiling people for their roles in our lives. We are looking for the right char-acteristics, background, education, experience and financial soundness and miss out on what miracles lay deep in the hearts of the desperate. Never under-estimate the fallen, the un-fit, and the overlooked because they just may be the missing ingredient to your lasting meal supply. Elijah could have pre-qualified this woman as not the right person for his provision, even though God was directed him to her. My guess is he would have died a hungry man and missed the ongoing ministry that God had for him. Folks, the proof is in the pudding. The plan of God always includes people who just don't fit. You see our thought process in evaluating is not always something we can fully trust. Add the guru's who instruct us on what the "right person" looks like, talks like and acts like and it may be the downfall of our hopes and dreams.

Perhaps this verse from I Corinthians 1:26-29 will be the inspiration for you to know that God wants you or someone else on the team. It says, "Take a good look, friends, at who you were when you got called into this life. I don't see many of the brightest and the best among you, not many influential, not many from high society families. Isn't it obvious that God deliberately chose men and women that the culture overlooks and exploits and abuses; chose these nobodies to expose the hollow pretensions of the "somebodies." Everything that we have—right thinking and right living, a clean slate and a fresh start—comes from God by way of Jesus Christ. That's why we have the saying, "If you're going to blow a horn, blow a trumpet for God (The Message)."

From one who blows a trumpet for God and speaks for all others who refuse to believe the ONE SIZE FITS ALL LIE let me say, you don't have to squeeze your head into a helmet that doesn't fit and live in pain the rest of your life to feel a part of the team. God has an answer that is tailored for you.

With this is mind, realize that network marketing is not for everyone, and just as being a captain on a boat, or a pastor, or a doctor or a singer is not for everyone. God made us all different, and the network marketing business is a special field and is not for everyone.

Although you may have evaluated a company, product or service, and compensation plan and have faith in it, just like sharing Christ, we are only the messengers, and we cannot prepare the heart of the listener. <u>Everyone will not fit into your business.</u> The sower is responsible for sowing the seed. The smart farmer will plant in fertilized and tilled soil. Some people will be open to your presentation immediately, some will listen and respond at a later time, some will listen and disregard, some will not even listen.

<u>Look for good soil.</u> Characteristics of great networkers are very similar to many of the spiritual gifts listed in Corinthians: wisdom, patience, faith and love. Look for those with the skills and desire to teach, lead, heal and communicate with others.

Avoid soil that is rocky, hard and dry. There are many people out there who are not made for network marketing as a business. There are individuals regardless of the positive evidence that will want nothing to do with networking because of their prior experiences or their "in the box" thinking. Move on from these individuals. Don't waste your time or energy.

There are other individuals who will be open to being customers of your product or service, but care nothing for the business. These consumers are typically a majority of your business and a foundation of your income.

Then there are those who will love your product or service, talk to a few other people about the business and build a small business.

Beyond these there will be people who see the business as a business. They will work to build the business and reap the rewards.

So who should you look for? All of these people. Don't discriminate. When you live your Christian witness, many will observe you, a few will have changed lives because of your witness. With wisdom and discernment plant your seeds by providing everyone with an introduction to your business. When the soil soaks in the seed, follow up, tend the soil, fertilize the soil, nurture the seed and see if it takes root to grow. This is where you want to spend your time, but remember don't just plant one seed. Continuously be planting, tending the seeds that have taken root and you will see a harvest.

If you find yourself planting and planting and not seeing a harvest, be sure you are working on your skills as a farmer. With your sponsor make sure you are not over watering, planting in the wrong spots, or putting out the wrong fertilizer. Keep in mind that this is a business and skill is required along with consistent effort. Not everyone will be successful in network marketing, just as not every student is successful in school, not every person is successful in their chosen profession. Many fail, but many also succeed.

James Allen posted these words on the calendar of time before he died. He said, "In all human affairs there are efforts and there are results, and the strength of the effort is the measure of the result." **Evaluate your circumstances, make God directed, wise decisions, look for human mentoring, plant seeds in good soil and persist.** A man can fail many times, but he isn't a failure until he gives up. You will reap if you faint not!

Chapter 11

I Stubbed My Toe
(Once in my business, how do I stay focused?)

"The art of being wise is the art of knowing what to overlook." – William James

I was awakened from a dead sleep in the middle of the night. No, it wasn't the fire alarm or the burglar alarm. It was the "get up and go to the bathroom" alarm, and I responded quickly. Half awake and half of me still in the grip of Mr. Sand Man, I managed to fall off the side of my bed and start the hazy journey to the bathroom. On my way, I stubbed my toe, and I must tell you, it hurt so badly that I almost forgot what I got up for in the first place.

Little things or big things can throw us off balance and cause us to lose sight of our goals. It happened to me on my way to the bathroom, but it has also happened in the business world. We stub our toe in network marketing and direct sales, and in the pain of the moment, we loose sight of our goal and an ocean of disappointment, discouragement and doubt floods our mind.

Human nature leans toward "getting sideways" when things don't go our way. The German contralto, Ernestine Schumann-Heink, was on her way to the platform when she collided with a music stand in the orchestra pit and sent music stands flying in every direction. The conductor quietly looked on with alarm and whispered to her, "Sideways, madam. Go sideways." The world famous contralto retorted, *"I have no sideways!"*

People who succeed in direct sales and network marketing must learn to avoid being turned sideways or upside down when toe-stubbing times come. Keep your eyes on your goal not the pain in your toe.

Paul did not allow "stubbed toes" to alter his course. He never got sideways with distractions that came his way. He rather said, **"So let's keep focused on that goal, those of us who want everything God has for us. If any of you have something else in mind, something less than total commitment, God will clear your blurred vision—-you'll see it yet! Now that we are on the right track, let's stay on it** (Philippians 3:13-14, The Message)."

Focus. Fervency. Faith. What a powerful combination. Never lose them. They are the ingredients of success. Abraham Lincoln had them and never allowed a few "toe stubbings" to prevent him from succeeding. Turn back a page or two in history and remember a few of the times he stubbed his toe on his way to phenomenal success.

- He failed miserably in his initial chosen profession of farming
- He fouled out in the business world
- The love of his life died, and he had a nervous breakdown
- Diphtheria took the life of his younger son
- He failed in his first bid for public office
- He failed in his first attempt to go to Congress
- He failed when he ran for the US senate
- He failed to gain the nomination for the vice-presidency of the USA

That guy with so many stubbed toes refused to give up, fought through hardship and failure and became one of the greatest and most revered presidents the United States has ever had. We remember him as the Great Emancipator, but what the world may not remember is that when he was sworn in as president of the most powerful nation in the world, high hat and all he was hiding stubbed toes underneath the leather of his polished shoes.

Nothing is said about what to do with a stubbed toe on the way to becoming successful, but it will happen. Paul doesn't overlook these tough times, but rather calls for toughness on our part. He said, *"Endure hardness, as a good soldier of Jesus Christ (II Timothy 2:3)."* It is recorded like this in The

Message. "When the going gets rough, take it on the chin with the rest of us, the way Jesus did."

Frank Leahy, the legendary football coach instilled this principle for winning into his football teams. He would tell them, "When the going gets tough, let the tough get going." He died in 1973, but his philosophy for winning lives on.

We need mental toughness in these tough economic times. It means that we need to have the ability to perform effectively despite the feelings and thoughts created by difficult circumstances. Otherwise, we will stub our toes and not know how to handle the pain.

Chester Nimitz prayed a prayer that expresses a need to the Father that affects us all. *"Grant me,"* I pray, *"the courage not to give up even though I think it is hopeless."* This is a tool that needs to be readily accessible to those of us who are engaged in network marketing. It's that special ability to keep going when we stub our toe and it hurts so badly we can hardly stand it.

If you are new to network marketing, you may not even know what to look for as potential problems, which will be equal to stubbing your toe. There are no less than eight such hazards that can affect your commitment to achieving success in your business.

Hazard Number 1: Buyer's remorse.

This is one of the first toe stubbing problems you will face. The excitement of the moment fades and reality sets in. The floodgates of questions swing open wide, and you question your own judgment.

"Did I make the right decision?" "Can I really do this?"

Sit back and take a deep breath. This is normal, but you must remember that you have invested in a BUSINESS. This is not a hobby. It is an honest effort to build an income that will accrue residual income streams. It will be working for me when I am asleep each night. Woody Allen expressed a thought, which can be applied to the stubbed toe of buyer's remorse. He wrote, "Eighty percent of success is showing up." You just showed up to begin a business, and that is the first step toward success.

To avoid this hazard work closely with your sponsor from day one, know the plan that will achieve reimbursement of your initial investment, the plan to receive your monthly automatic order free and know the plan that will bring you into prof-itability. Every compensation plan is different. You want consistent guidance and clear direction in the beginning to achieve signups and in some compen-sation plans the optimal placement of your new sign ups. This eliminates the financial risk and dismisses buyer's remorse.

Hazard number 2: The loss of your security blanket.

There is no real security in this world. Many people are looking at tough economic times and real-izing that as fact. The Bible is not silent about false security. In Timothy 6:17 we are warned against "trusting UNCERTAIN riches, but in the living God, who giveth us richly all things to enjoy..." Riches come. Riches go, but God remains. Trust Him. These economic times are truly an opportunity for Christians to share with others the security we have in Christ regardless of circumstances.

For most individuals today financial security is found in a nine to five job and a steady paycheck. But, if you are reading this book you are looking for more, for some reason, whether it is the desire or need for additional income, the desire or need for freedom to work from home or the desire or need to do something for others. Whatever the reason, if you have never worked a home based business where you are in charge of your schedule, actions, and paycheck, than the loss of security can be frightening.

Take the security blanket away from a child, and you will have an unhappy camper on your hands. Now, let's face it. That security blanket can do nothing more than keep them warm, but it feels good to them. It's false security in reality that can be jerked away from them at any moment. Ask the 1,000,000 people in North America that started a small business last year. 800,000 of them will fold in the first five years. Of those 200,000 that make it past five years, 160,000 will fail in the next five years. These are facts that I obtained from Michael Gerber who is the author of the E-Myth in 2008.

Do not let these statistics hold you back, let them strengthen you. If you go into a business knowing the odds, then they will not surprise you or hold you back and you will be grounded to face the odds and to be one of the many successes. The wonderful thing about network marketing is regardless of the initial cost and the monthly automatic order; this is an industry that provides you with a dramatically low start up cost to own your own business with potential for greater payoff.

To avoid stubbing your toe on this one, maintain your primary income while building your income to the level it supplements and then replaces your current income. This business can be built around your current commitments. To achieve success quickly we highly recommend committing a minimum of 10 hours per week to your business. Getting momentum started and replacement of your initial investment is critical to feeling secure with your decision.

Hazard number 3: The doubting debacle

Watch out for that rock of doubt. You can stub your toe there. Avoid it. Go over it. Go around it. Go through it.

Never put a question mark where God has put a period. The Bible tells us that "All the promises of God in Him are yeah, and in Him Amen (II Corinthians 1:20)." When I cannot trust my feeling, I can with confidence trust His Word.

Overcome doubt through building your confidence in the industry, company, product, service and the opportunity you choose. This is where your support systems are crucial. Talk with them, do calls with them, follow their lead. As you build your own team, doubts will dwindle. If you have been on your knees regarding the decision to commit yourself to your business and you know it is right for you, then do not let Satan or anyone else introduce doubts into your mind.

Hazard number 4: Confidence in the industry, company, product or service quivers

This toe stubbing takes a heavy toll upon "newbies" as well as pros, because it shakes the foundations of what you have established your belief and invested your time and money in. Many networkers, just like other business owners, will experience times when confidence will be shaken. Companies falter, compensation plans change, sponsors and distributors slack off or leave.

When you look at the industry as a whole you will see that there are a mix of individuals that have been successful in the industry. Some have been with companies for a long time and built large faithful followings, some have experienced the exact right company at the exact right time and created grand incomes overnight, some have skills that have allowed them to be successful in several companies. The description of success in this context is reimbursement of initial investment, free monthly products or services and a minimum of $3,000 a month in residual income. By residual I mean it keeps coming monthly. Regardless of how they became successful, what you will see with these individuals is that few of them will leave the industry regardless of what happens because they have experienced success and believe that this industry provides unlimited potential.

When confidence quivers, your fortitude is what will take you far beyond this hazard. When something arises that causes you to question, stay calm, ask questions, pray and make good decisions. If you have been faithful to your sponsors (upline) and the people you have sponsored or that have been sponsored below you (downline) then you will survive one way or another.

I am a firm believer that the individual who is driven by the desire to succeed will find a way. Philippians 1:27-28 says

"Stand united, singular in vision, contending for people's trust in the Message, the good news, not flinching or dodging in the slightest before the opposition. Your courage and unity will show them what they're up against; defeat for them, victory for you——both because of God (The Message).*"*

Hazard number 5: The quick fix pothole

Network marketing success doesn't just happen overnight. If you are searching to get rich quick, in all honesty, you need to be looking somewhere else. This "ain't" it. This is not a get rich quick scheme as many people will say, it is a legitimate business built upon the ordering of a product or service and the sponsoring of others and development of leaders. Depending on the compensation plan, return on investment may occur fast or slow, but it definitely requires your investment of time and effort.

The way to avoid this pothole is easy. Apply correct business principles and exercise a good work ethic. Make a commitment and stick with it. It is *"commitment that unlocks the doors of imagination, allows vision, and gives us the right stuff to turn our dreams into reality'* so said James Womack.

Hazard number 6: The emotional roller coaster shock

There are ups and downs in business as well as life. It is like the tide. Having chosen this business as a business, realize that it requires sharing, selling, mentoring, educating, recruiting, helping, encouraging, and loving what you do! It is normal for the tide to come in and go out. It goes out, but you can also count on it to come back in. I appreciate the admission of the Psalmist to the highs and lows that he had in life. In Psalms 40:1 he described a terrible low time in his life. He said, *"He brought me up also out of a horrible pit, out of the miry clay, and set my feet upon a rock, and established my goings. And he has put a new song in my mouth..."* He was down but not out. He described his dilemma as being not just in a pit but in a horrible pit. From the way he describes it, he was stuck there, but God pulled him out and not only just his head above the edge, but He gave him a new song in his heart.

God has a song to replace your shock. You can't avoid this roller coaster shock, but you can survive it. Network marketing businesses grow as the product, service or opportunity is shared. If you are sharing what you have with people every day, every week, every month, etc... then you will find people who desire what you have. The more prospects you have, the less you are impacted if one person says they are not interested. The more people in your down line and the greater your income the less you are impacted by normal fluctuations in the business. Commit consistently to your business and you will love the roller coaster ride, not give into the shock.

Hazard number 7: The looking back danger

Looking back is dangerous if you are moving forward. It prevents you from seeing what is ahead whether good or bad.

Regardless of your experiences with the industry to date, the decisions you make today and what you do today and tomorrow are what will make the difference in whether you succeed in your business and achieve the goals you are reaching for.

Hazard number 8: The irrational thinking trap

Network marketing, like the church, seems to be an open invitation to those who are passionate and committed, to those who are lukewarm and to those who couldn't see their way out of a door if you pushed them. Far too often, people with screwed up thinking will say that they just can't do this or that they are not cut out for network marketing and honestly many are not. Two little words throw a wrench into their wheels of progress. Those words are: I can't.

Arguably, the network marketing industry has their share of messed up thinkers who are proud members of the "I can't" fraternity. They are brain washed into believing that they can't sell. They can't prospect. They can't follow a blue print to success and yet most of them are incredibly convincing when they tell everybody about their favorite movie and their favorite restaurant.

More people have stubbed their toe here than in other areas of their personal development. It would have been easy for the guest at the wedding where the bride and groom were embarrassed to tears when they ran out of refreshments to say "the party is over", but instead water pots were carried to Jesus, and He did the rest. The best wine was then served.

To avoid the irrational thinking trap be realistic, level headed, committed and consistent. When you turn your "cant's" over to God, He will miraculously turn them into "cans."

- God can give you favor with people. (Proverbs 3:3-4)
- God can lead you to be in the right place at the right time to meet the right people. (Psalms 37:23)
- God can put words in your mouth at the appropriate moment. (Matthew 10:19-20)
- God can cause you to succeed beyond your wildest dreams. (Ephesians 3:20)
- I am a child of the King. My Father owns the cattle on a thousand hills and watches over the sparrow and the flowers in the fields, certainly He will watch over me.

Make the turn right now and decide to make the "I can" confession. Say it orally. "I can do all things through Christ which strengthens me (Philippians 4:13)."

Don't stump your toe on "I can't." It's the devil's lie, and you must not believe it.

Hazard number 9: The rejection trauma

All marketing is a numbers game. Each "no" brings you closer to a "yes". It's not your pride that is at stake. It's your financial future. Rejections hurt, but you must not allow them to hurt your vision, ditch your hopes, sink your enthusiasm or blind you to your opportunities.

Ralph Waldo Emerson's words should encourage you to face rejection as the rain pounds down on a duck's back. The water runs off the backs of our feathered friends, but does not get inside. It's the way God made them. He expressed it with these fantastic words, *"What lies behind us and what lies before us are small matters compared to what lies within us."*

Surviving rejection initially is the hardest part because until you have your initial return on investment and until you have experienced the product or service benefits for yourself, even a comment, look, or a question you may not know the answer to, can feel like rejection. Initially, work with your sponsor and support systems, they will get you through this initial period, and as mentioned earlier run the numbers.

Before you even begin realize that like any business or career, this will not be for everyone. Don't spend your time focusing on one person, set your goals to talk to as many as possible. Don't let a day go by when you don't "work" your business. You are a business owner. People will come in and go out of your doors, and that's O.K. Some of them will purchase and some will not. Look beyond rejection, pray and persist. As the duck would say, "Let the rain come."

Compile a "DON'T DO" list as an effective counterpunch to rejection.

We have been taught with dogged persistence to make a "To Do" list and follow it judiciously. But how many of us have been taught to compile a "DON'T DO" list to guide us through the terrifying waters of rejection? I dare say few if any.

Your upline, downline and sideline should take a pro-active position in doing it quickly. My "DON'T DO" list looks like this. Copy it or compile your own, but just do it! "A prudent man foresees the difficulties ahead and prepares for them; the simpleton goes blindly on and suffers the consequences (Proverbs 22:3, The Living Bible)."

1. Don't beat yourself up. It will be hazardous to your emotional health.
2. Don't spend the time and energy on worrying. It will be counter productive. The Bible has 365 scriptures discouraging worry. One for every day of your life and business.

3. Don't attempt to reinvent the wheel. The system in place is effective. Others have done it, so can you.

4. Don't analyze until you are fossilized. Over analyzing can be agonizing and an excuse for inactivity in advancing your business.

5. Don't host a pity party. If you must have pity on something or someone, have pity on the customer who passed on a golden opportunity.

6. Don't assume that failure is final. Rejections are not failures if they provoke you to rethink, re-conceptualize and re-strategize. Remind yourself of those who have been rejected repeatedly and yet are some of the greatest in history including Jesus.

7. Don't attempt to make critical decisions when you are on the rebound from a rejection trauma.

8. Don't forget past victories. You may have lost one battle, but you are going to win the war... and to the victor goes the spoils.

The Bible tells us in no uncertain terms that God who is IN us is greater than any adversary we face including rejection (I John 4:4). Don't settle for too little or nothing at all. God wants you to have the best.

Chapter 12

Understanding the Mathematics of the Business

II Corinthians 9:6 "He which soweth sparingly shall reap also sparingly; and he which soweth bountifully shall reap also bountifully."

Did you ever wonder why so many different people with so many different personalities, interests and mental abilities all are processed through schools that teach a standard set of subjects including reading, science, writing, language, and math? Why do people who will be scientists need to know where a comma goes? Why do people who will be math teachers need to know what pie means? Why do professional athletes need to read? It's because knowledge bases overlap. We don't know who will develop into what. So our educational system provides every student with a base format of learning. As we well know, some respond well and excel, some meet the guidelines, some barely get by and struggle, some can't or won't do it and drop out of the system.

Network marketing is a similar scenario. It is available to the masses because of its large volume of companies, its relatively low start up and maintenance cost, and it is based on the same principles even though it may be presented in different ways by different companies. The courses in network marketing are the same: know the company, know the product or service, know the compensation plan, learn to contact, share and recruit, learn to develop your organization. Because of our differences some of us relate better to some subjects and some of us relate to others, some excel, some just get by and some fall out.

One of the classes required in network marketing is Math. We've broken it down into Math 101, 201 and 301. For those of you like me, don't get scared. It is simple math, but oh so critical to belief, so welcome back to the math class that pays.

Math 101: Geometric Progression

Belief in the network marketing industry is based on the understanding of a mathematical fact called geometric progression. Once you understand geometric progression you will believe your potential is undeniable. The reason that network marketing is also called multi-level marketing is because it is based on building a progressive network of individuals that multiply themselves. Do the math, as you bring in people and each of them brings in people your efforts are multiplied. If you bring in one person that brings in one, you have two. If you bring in two people who bring in two, now you have four. 3 x 3 = 9. 10 x 10 = 100. In standard businesses you must reach a manager level or franchise before your efforts multiply into profits. In network marketing it begins the day you teach your first person to sign up a new distributor.

One of the many advantages of network marketing math is that of the automatic order. In standard sales for example working in a store, real estate, or provision of a service like doctor's visits, salon visits, plumbing etc., once you complete a sale, you are unemployed until your next sale or appointment unless you are receiving overrides. Only select sales opportunities such as network marketing provide repeat and residual income so you are receiving ongoing income based on your initial sales efforts. Remember geometric progression. As it continues paychecks increase accordingly.

Math 201: Categories and Percentages

Understanding the five categories of people you will work with in your network marketing business will increase the rate of your geometric progression.

Category 1: Customers with NO interest in working the business but love and order the product/service each month. Your customers are your bread and butter and provide you with much of your income.

Category 2: Casual networkers who have some desire, but no consistent time or commitment to build their business. Be sure to work with these networkers until they earn enough money to pay for their products. Help them anytime they have a new prospect and sometimes they will surprise you and build a steady small business. They may become more serious later as they receive slowly increasing checks, as their success with the products/service is experienced and as you expand their vision.

Category 3: Mom and Pop networkers love the product/service and the idea of a home-based business. They work to achieve $500 to $2,500 a month, but usually work in spells to achieve it. They usually are not willing to make big changes in lifestyle or commit consistently day in and day out to advance. Here is the math around ninety-five percent of your business may fall into categories 1, 2 and 3.

Category 4: Professional networkers desperately want more out of life and have a burning desire to achieve success in this industry. They apply themselves consistently with recruitment and training until they reach over $3,000 a month in residual income. They envision and often achieve $10,000, $20,000, or $50,000 or more a month.

Category 5: Seasoned networkers are people from Group 4 that have reached a rock solid belief in themselves and network marketing. They have reached over $10,000 a month in residual income and they continue to recruit, train and develop their organizations. The industry and companies boast of these individuals with million dollar plus earnings. Most solid companies have these success stories and we can all learn from their experiences. Many of them started just like you with the desire to improve their lives one step at a time. The difference in them and you is likely only to be when they got started and their consistency of effort over time.

To achieve geometric progression at a rapid rate develop each of these five types of networkers in your business and you will be on your path to reaching category 4 and 5.

Math 301: The Power of Momentum and Return on Investment

Network marketing can offer returns on your investment that few other business opportunities can offer! Action creates enthusiasm and excitement. Your enthusiasm is a fire, which can either ignite or melt the possibilities! Being lukewarm about what you are doing will never change anyone, nor multiply your efforts. Being on fire about your opportunity causes people to believe. If they catch your fire, they will do the business with you. The result is duplication and substantial growth. Successful prospecting is 90% enthusiasm and 10% knowledge. The key is to maintain this ratio as you learn more and as your business expands. Light a fire of enthusiasm and people will come from miles to watch it burn.

It's just like a locomotive on a track. It is dreadfully slow as the wheels begin to turn, but once the power and momentum take over, it takes thousands of pounds of brake power to make it stop. Geometric progression in network marketing might be slow to get rolling but once you get momentum, it is hard to stop. So how do you get and sustain the momentum? 1. Make contacts every day until you reach momentum, 2. Do follow-ups to sustain the momentum and 3. Keep prospecting to increase it.

Return on investment and the rate that you will receive that return is strongly based on the guidance you receive, your companies' compensation plan, your ability to make contacts and your ability to train others to duplicate your efforts.

Chapter 13

Strengthening Your Core,
Relationships can make or break your business

Ecclesiastes 4:9 "Two are better than one; because they have a good reward for their labor."

In your search for riches, don't lose the things that money can't buy.

If you have ever worked out, been with a physical trainer, had a back injury or had difficulty with your balance, you may have heard your instructor say, "We need to work on your core strength". This 'core' is a group of stabilizing muscles that supports the body for many key activities including standing, bending, walking, balancing, etc...

In network marketing, also known as relationship marketing because success is largely based on your

ability to achieve, maintain and develop relationships, you must strengthen your core relationships.
You will find that if you focus on this aspect of the
business that you will enjoy the business, bring joy
to yourself and others and become successful. What
many in the industry fail to do causing destruction of
the unlimited opportunity of this industry is they get
their relationship priorities out of order.

**Our relationship with God must come first
and foremost. As a Christian walks he/she must
keep relationships in order.** The Bible is very clear
and we offer only a few of the relationship scriptures
here that directly influence our network marketing
businesses.

- Deuteronomy 8:16-18 (The Open Bible New
  American Standard) "In the wilderness He
  fed you manna which your fathers did not
  know, that He might humble you and that **He
  might test you, to do good for you in the
  end**. Otherwise, you may say in your heart,
  'My power and the strength of my hand made
  me this wealth.' "But you shall remember the
  Lord your God, **for it is He who is giving you
  power to make wealth** that He may confirm
  His covenant which He swore to your fathers,
  as it is this day."
- Exodus 20: 3 (The Living Bible) "You shall
  have **no other gods** before Me."
- Proverbs 3: 9-10 (The Living Bible) "Honor
  the Lord by giving Him **the first part of all
  your income**, and he will fill your barns with

wheat and barley and overflow your wine vats with the finest wines."

- Proverbs 10: 22 (The Living Bible) "**The Lord's blessing** is our greatest wealth. All our work adds nothing to it!"
- Proverbs 10:27 (The Living Bible) "Reverence for God adds hours to each day"
- Proverbs 13:13 (The Living Bible) "Despise God's Word and find yourself in trouble. Obey it and succeed."
- (The Living Bible) Proverbs 16:1 "We can make our plans, but the final outcome is in God's hands."
- (The Living Bible) Proverbs 16:3 "Commit your work to the Lord, then it will succeed."
- (The Living Bible) Proverbs 16:9 "We should make plans-counting on God to direct us.

Family relationships

Without our relationships with family and friends, money cannot bring joy. If you doubt this, look to Hollywood relationships where multi-million dollar marriages fall apart frequently. Nothing is more common and important to our lives than the family and we must consider that being a Christian does not eliminate this problem. We know by recent statistics that the divorce rate in the churches rivals that in the secular community and often financial stress is an impacting factor.

Lyndon Baines Johnson, former president of the United States, held the family in highest esteem. Of it he said, *"The family is the corner stone of our society.*

More than any other force it shapes the attitude, the hopes, the ambitions, and the values of the child... So, unless we work to strengthen the family...all the rest—-schools, playgrounds, and public assistance, and private concern——will never be enough."

Since the family is the cornerstone of society and civilization, network marketers must learn to arrange the priorities correctly in their lives. The family MUST NEVER be an appendage to your business. They must be part and parcel of making it work for the good of the home.

Absence does not make the heart grow fonder when business becomes the rival to family time and relationships. In that event, absence can breed bitterness and resentments. It is up to you to include them in your decision making, ask for their emotional support if nothing else, communicate your goals, plans and schedule and celebrate your successes with them. As you ask them to support you be sure to

- Communicate clearly
- Express your love to them sincerely
- Laugh with them frequently
- Value their opinions continually
- Express an interest in what they are doing eagerly
- Dedicate time to spend with them lovingly
- Learn to listen to their heart as well as their words honestly
- Determine a manageable business budget consistently

"In family life, love is the oil that eases friction, the cement that binds closer together, and the music that brings harmony," so declares Eva Burrows.

The widow in I Kings 17 was one of many single parents who have carried the load of raising a family alone. She received a supernatural miracle. We must not put ourselves in the mindset that a supernatural miracle is going to be produced because we sign up in a network marketing business.

Many have failed in network marketing and broken down relationships with family and friends because they entered it in a time of crisis and put an unrealistically high demand for immediate income on themselves, their prospects, the company, the compensation plan and their sponsors. Hence, statements like "Network marketing doesn't work." "I tried it and I didn't make any money." "It's a scam."

When beginning this business or any other realize that you should have something to pay the bills in the beginning or have something to fall back on. We discussed geometric progression and how it works. Unless you are a dynamic, go getter, with a lot of contacts or the God given ability to make friends and influence people at dramatic rates, then income in the first 30 days sufficient to pay the bills or replace your current income is unlikely.

If you are in the position of needing money immediately, don't let this hold you back. Find your immediate source and find a sponsor who will work with you along the lines you have learned in this book to create your secondary income. Work at least ten to fifteen hours a week and get to work on your dream.

I know this can be done, because it has already been done by many.

It is never recommend that you quit an income job to start a commission job unless your knowledge and skills can propel you to success quickly. This immediately causes undo stress on yourself, the success that is possible from your new business and on your personal relationships. Begin your relationship as a business owner with honest expectations for yourself and you will increase your potential for staying the course and achieving full-time income dramatically.

Enrich your family first, then conquer the business world and take it by a storm. It is the strategy to synergize without compromise.

Relationships with your company, sponsor, down line and customers

A nebulous pie in the sky would mean nothing to the widow if she could not feed her son and prevent him from dying from malnutrition. James must have had this concept in mind when he wrote, *"Dear friends, do you think you'll get anywhere in this if you learn all the right words but never do anything? Does merely talking about faith indicate that a person really has it? For instance, you come upon an old friend dressed in rags and half-starved and say, Good morning, friend! Be clothed...and walk off without providing so much as a coat or a cup of soup——where does that get you? Isn't it obvious that God-talk without God acts is outrageous nonsense (James 2:14-18, The Message)?"*

Andrew Carnegie knew what he was talking about when he suggested that *"No man can become rich without himself enriching others."*

The Bible also gives us clear direction in this area:

- (The Living Bible) Proverbs 10:14 A wise man holds his tongue. Only a fool blurts out everything he knows; that only leads to sorrow and trouble.
- (The Living Bible) Proverbs 13:17 "An unreliable messenger can cause a lot of trouble. Reliable communication permits progress."
- (The Living Bible) Proverbs 12:15 "A fool thinks he needs no advice, but a wise man listens to others.
- (The Living Bible) Proverbs 13:18-20 "If you refuse criticism you will end in poverty and disgrace; if you accept criticism you are on the road to fame. It is pleasant to see plans develop. That is why fools refuse to give them up even when they are wrong. Be with wise men and become wise. Be with evil men and become evil."
- (The Living Bible) Proverbs 16:11 "The Lord demands fairness in every business deal. He established this principle."
- (The Living Bible) Proverbs 21:5 "Steady plodding brings prosperity; hasty speculation brings poverty."

Knute Rockne, Notre Dame's legendary football coach is quoted as saying, "An automobile goes nowhere efficiently unless it has a quick, hot spark to ignite things, to set the cogs of the machine in motion. So I try to make every player on my team feel he's the spark keeping our machine in motion. On him depends our success."

If you treat each of your family and downline like they are the vital spark in your business and they are special to you, then you will keep your business in motion. When you bring someone into your downline, whether it is to purchase a product or service, or to build a financial dream, then they have demonstrated trust in what you have said. Be honest, caring, sincere, and maintain contact. If you honestly and sincerely let them know you appreciate them, that you care about their satisfaction, and that you will help them meet their needs, then you will be on your way to a successful network marketing business.

Success can be defined as being uncommonly good in taking care of the most common things!

Network marketers must come to grips with real problems not hyperboles. We must synergize to bring hope. Use your position and influence in the business world to make a positive impact upon the world. John Wesley penned these eloquent words to challenge all of us to use our position and influence to improve the quality of life for all those whose lives we touch. He encouraged us to: *"do all the good you can, by all the means you can, in all the ways you can, in all the places you can, at all the times you can, to all the people you can, as long as ever you can."*

Jesus assigned meaning to the value of influence when he taught these words. *"You are the light of the world. A city that is set on a hill cannot be hid. Neither do men light a candle, and put it under a bushel, but on a candlestick; and it giveth light unto all that are in the house. Let your light so shine before men, that they may see your good works, and glorify your Father which is in heaven (Matthew 5:14-16)."*

Network marketers have a story to tell, a hope to bring, an opportunity to share and a friendship to give. We must not keep silent nor go it alone. We stand together united for a cause, and in unity we have synergy. What I can do, plus what God can do, equals enough.

"No one can possibly achieve any real and lasting success or 'get rich' in business by being a conformist." — J. Paul Getty

Chapter 14

Re-packaged, Re-think, Re-do

"Freedom lies in being bold."
— Robert Frost

Ephesians 3:20 "Now unto him that is able to do exceeding abundantly above all that we ask or think, according to the power that worketh in us."

When the brook dries up, it is time to resist conformity and think outside the box. Elijah did, and it proved to be miraculous for him.

Elijah had boldness when his back was forced against the wall and he realized that he had no water, no ravens, and no provisions. No matter how many different ways he made a positive confession, or how many blood drops of sweat flowed down his face from days of prayer, the brook dried up and it was time for him to activate a new plan of action and allow new ideas to crop up in his head.

Victor Hugo reminds us of the power of new ideas. He wrote, *"There is one thing stronger than all the armies in the world: an idea whose time has come."*

My friend, Bob Guess and author of the book – *Some rob you with a Pen,* declared that your own financial destiny will be determined "by knowledge (what to do), the confidence (when to do it) and the wisdom (with whom to do it)." And it all starts with a simple idea whose time has come.

Interestingly enough Elijah had such an idea, but he did not do what many of us might have done when it became evident that his resources for survival were drying up. He didn't go into denial and fight reality by digging harder, wider, or even deeper hoping to turn the tide by striking an artesian well.

Elijah bit the bullet, pulled the plug and decided to let go of the familiar and take hold of an untried challenge, which lay ahead. God often uses unfortunate and unfavorable situations to nudge us into a different direction and fuel our minds with new ideas. Such ideas are seldom comfortable to initiate and almost always revolutionary in their outcome.

Sometimes one of the hardest things to do is to leave a place that has been so productive to us for so long. It's revolting and revolutionary. All that was familiar and cozy to him were jerked out from under him the moment the brook dried up. We can't pinpoint how long Elijah had been sustained and made secure by the brook but we are certain when he left. It was at the moment that his brook went dry. The squeeze was on. The handwriting was on the wall, and his economic world crashed all around him.

Put this down in your day timer, and don't forget it. **We learn something from prosperity, but we learn much more from adversity**. Elijah learned to trust God in adversity and to proceed as if he knew he could not fail. He didn't waste a lot of time consulting committees, or even taking a couple of days to pray about it.

Warren Buffet didn't mince words when he said, "When you find yourself in a hole, the best thing you can do is stop digging." Elijah, the prophet of God, was in a hole, and he stopped digging. When his provisions failed, he kept his eyes on the Provider and not upon the medium of the provision. The Bible makes it clear that *"My God shall supply all your need according to his riches in glory by Christ Jesus* (Philippians 4:19)." J. Sidlow Baxter broke this Scripture down so beautifully in his book, *His Part and Ours*.

He maintains that the Provider gives us a 7-fold explanation of our supply.

- The source of the supply – "my God"
- The certainty of the supply – "shall"
- The fullness of the supply – "fulfill" (R.V.)
- The extent of the supply – "all your need"
- The measure of the supply – "according to His riches"
- The storehouse of the supply – "in glory"

- And the medium of the supply – "in Christ Jesus."

Cherith was only a place where God had provided for Him. The true security was not in the place or even the brook, but in The Provider. Moses knew the security of having the Provider with him in every circumstance in life. So adamant was he about having the Provider with him that he cried out to God, *"If thy presence go not with me, carry us not hence (Exodus 33:15)."*

Elijah kept his eyes on the Provider when Cherith faded out of view; and hard as I try, I can't find any tears of remorse or bitter cries of desperation in the entire episode. He displays no sign of worrying, no fretting, and no loss of sleep at night. With the Provider by his side and leading the way, he checks out and is gone like hopping an early morning freight train and leaving town to tackle his new challenge and does not seem to ever look longingly back.

You don't ever hear him say, "I gave my life to that brook or I spent the best years of my life here and look what it has done for me." In other words, you can take away a job, but you can't take away someone's spirit. Whether intentionally or unintentionally, good or bad the brook was never mentioned again. That chapter of his life was closed. Why? The brook had served its purpose nothing more, nothing less. *Mercifully he understood the place of provision is interchangeable but the Provider is the constant.*

Many because of loss of jobs, loss of benefits, and loss of titles are suffering shame. Ask yourself this question, "What am I going to learn about myself in this situation?" **Our strengths and our weakness are most evident when we are in crisis. You have a choice of whether to look back, remain in the status quo or move forward.**

The brook was a page of the past and had no place in Elijah's future. He planned no homecomings to honor the brook, no monuments were erected in its name, and not one street was dedicated to its memory. The place of the provision changed and since Elijah was not married to the place but completely committed to the Provider it was easier to walk away and try something different.

What is your brook that is hard for you to give up and walk away from? Is it the "daily bread and butter" to keep you and your family alive? Is it the steady paycheck? The two weeks of vacation with pay? The 401 K that is a nest egg for retirement security? Please be careful that your eyes do not become fixated on the place because it may well change without notice, but your Provider has the situation that you will be facing under control. Paul gave us this admonition in I Timothy 6: 17. *"Charge them that are rich in this world, that they be not high minded, nor trust in uncertain riches, but in the living God, who giveth us richly all things to enjoy."* Riches come and riches go, but God remains ever the same! God is, God was, and God will evermore be God. Trust Him. He will not fail you. It is time now for you to re-think, re-package and re-do the things you have done to date if you want to see yourself in this industry achieving great things.

159

We, the church, are to be a beacon shining brightly into the dark world of sin and despair, but may it also be a shining light pointing men and women to financial opportunities that they have not discovered in the want ads, the unemployment office or in government stimulus plans. May we provide them with opportunities for gainful employment!

A recent survey of National Association of Church Business Administration members found that 32% said their church had financial difficulties. This percentage has rocketed by 14% in 2009 alone.

It is interesting to see how Paul handled such matters in II Corinthians 9:8, 10. He wrote these classic words. "God can pour on the blessings in astonishing ways so that you're ready for anything and everything, more than just ready to do what needs to be done...The most generous GOD WHO GIVES SEED to the farmer that becomes bread for your meals is more than extravagant with you. He gives you something you can then give away... (The Message)"

There may be a thousand ways in which God gives seed to the farmer to put beans and potatoes on the table, and network marketing just might be one of them. It's not a government hand out plan or entitlement program. It's a legitimate, honest way to earn a living.

Everywhere Jesus went, He brought hope. For the sick, he brought hope of healing. For the down and out, he brought hope of recovery. For the storm tossed, He brought hope or security. For professional fishermen who had not earned a dime to show for their untiring efforts, He brought hope to turn a profit before they pulled in their nets.

John records the hope that Jesus, the carpenter's son, brought to the seaside where disappointed professional fishermen were about to call it a night. They had fished all night and had nothing, absolutely nothing to show for it except nasty nets and sore, swollen muscles. Then this carpenter's son shows up and gives them a bit of unwelcome advice. They probably chafed in disgust because the pros were being told how to succeed after a night of failure from a guy who didn't have a cane fishing pole in his hand. It was humiliating, but they listened.

His advice was simple and straightforward. "Cast your nets on the right side of the ship, and you shall find. They cast therefore, and now they were not able to draw it for the multitude of fishes (John 21:6)." They didn't need a financial consultant or adjustment to their budget. *They needed to make a minor adjustment that made a major difference* and their short fall was turned to abundance.

Jesus brought hope to the work place and affected their bank account. The Good Shepherd was not only involved in their eternal destiny but in helping them to have a roof over their head, food on the table and money to pay their bills. He provided a plan for them to meet a tax obligation that was coming due shortly and they lacked funds for paying it. He didn't just give them a hand out. He gave them a job and assumed the responsibility of making sure that they would succeed.

He knows and understands what it is really like to depend upon God totally for His daily necessities. The Good, Chief Shepherd is and ever will be "touched with the feelings of our infirmities (Hebrews 4:15)."

Please, let me make this perfectly clear. No one is saying that everything done in the name of network marketing is without blemish, but neither should it be said that all are one and the same. Old traditional brooks are drying up on every hand, and the daily headlines leave this debate without argument. However, I am not pretending to surmise that everyone is going to find the new place of provision in network marketing, absolutely not, but if you have picked this book up, then know that regardless of what men may say, this industry may be your next brook, river, or ocean of opportunity.

I regularly turn to Galatians 6:1-2 for my own edification and instruction. It reminds us to: "Live creatively. If someone falls into sin, forgivingly restore him, saving your critical comments for yourself. You might be needing forgiveness before the day is out. Stoop down and reach out to those who are oppressed. Share their burdens, and so complete Christ's law. If you think you are too good for that, you are deceived (The Message)."

Live creatively and pray sincerely!

- Pray for alternative sources of income for the tither.
- Pray that God will teach us to profit. (Isaiah 48:17)

- Pray that believers will abound with blessings. (Proverbs 28:20)
- Pray that the poverty mentality will disappear and abundance mentality will appear.
- Pray that believers will refuse to be caught up in impulse spending.
- Pray that dead revenue streams will have a glorious resurrection.
- Pray that God will give us creative wealth producing ideas.
- Pray for raises in salaries, bonus checks and even stock options.
- Pray for promotions and job security
- Pray for a hedge of protection over our finances, homes, and relationships
- Pray that the network marketing opportunity will be considered seriously and not with doubting and trepidation.
- Pray that believers will focus on the Provider and not the medium of provision.

In summary, let me encourage you to draw strength and wisdom through the benefits of prayer because prayer is...

- The prelude to peace
- The prologue to power
- The preface to purpose
- And the pathway to perfection.

We may not know what the future holds, but we know who holds the future, and we

are not afraid to step out in faith and to trust the unknown future to our known God. May you find peace, joy and God's blessings. Amen.

Printed in the United States
152031LV00001B/1/P